GIVING IT ALL AWAY

THE DORIS BUFFETT STORY

GIVING IT ALL AWAY

THE DORIS BUFFETT STORY

MICHAEL ZITZ

THE PERMANENT PRESS
Sag Harbor, NY 11963

For information, address:
The Permanent Press
4170 Noyac Road
Sag Harbor, NY 11963
www.thepermanentpress.com

Library of Congress Cataloging-in-Publication Data

Zitz, Michael—
    Giving it all away : the Doris Buffett story / Michael Zitz.
        p. cm.
    ISBN 978-1-57962-209-1 (hardcover : alk. paper)
        1. Buffett, Doris, 1928– 2. Buffett, Doris, 1928—Political and social views. 3. Buffett, Doris, 1928—Family. 4. Women philanthropists—United States—Biography. 5. Social reformers—United States—Biography. 6. Sunshine Lady Foundation. 7. Civic leaders—Virginia—Fredericksburg—Biography. 8. Buffett, Warren—Family. 9. Buffett, Howard, 1903–1964—Family. 10. Fredericksburg (Va.)—Biography. I. Title.

CT275.B78483Z58 2010
361.7'4092—dc22
[B]   2010006409

Printed in the United States of America.

To Jean Boswell Oravits

Contents

$\mathscr{P}$HOTOS

$\mathscr{A}$CKNOWLEDGEMENTS

$\mathscr{I}$'d like to thank Warren Buffett, God, and my wife, Lisa Ferreira.

After our first interview for this book, Doris Buffett and I walked out onto the sidewalk outside her 230-year-old home in Fredericksburg, Virginia and a woman pushing a baby carriage craned her neck and said, "Aren't you Warren Buffett's sister?" I joked that when this book was published, someone would ask Warren, "Aren't you Doris Buffett's brother?"

A writer can't ask for anything more than a good story to tell. Doris is a great one—perhaps even a better story than her brother. I hope this book comes close to doing that story justice. Simply being around her is an uplifting experience. Her excitement about life, her insatiable curiosity, her eagerness to learn, her desire to help others and her laughter are infectious. It's my hope that learning about the things she has overcome and the positive, caring attitude she has managed to maintain about the world will inspire those who believe they can't pick themselves up and go on, as well as those who think they can't make a difference.

There are no words to thank her for her trust in me and her willingness to open up and talk about things that were painful to recall and that she had understandable reluctance to share with the world. She did so in the hope that talking about the effect mental illness and emotional abuse have on families might help ease the stigma attached to treatment and let victims know it is possible to find happiness. To paraphrase a line from *The Bucket List*, "I'm deeply proud that this woman found it worth her while to know me."

My publishers, Judith and Martin Shepard, and my editors, Karen Owen and Joslyn Pine, deserve great credit for their wisdom, guidance, patience and hard work. I'd also like to thank Paula Raudenbush and Susan Ahlquist for their help in editing the photographs in this book. Some of the images of the Buffetts have never been published before.

My young sons, Robbie and Jay, deserve medals for their patience during the months their dad was either traveling, on the phone or hunched over a keyboard shushing them. When six-year-old Jay heard Dad was doing a book about the woman he calls Dodo, his eyes widened. Moments later he handed me a drawing of a stick figure of me with my arms extended as dollar bills fluttered down from the sky. "Dad, you're going to make *ten hundred dollars* on this book!" he exclaimed.

Warren helped me tell Doris' story by writing the Foreward for this book and generously giving of his time for interviews. Other family members—Alexander Buffett Rozek, Robin Wood, Marshall Wood and Bertie Buffett Elliott—provided invaluable insight.

At the Sunshine Lady Foundation, Peggy Altman, Diane Grimsley, Mitty Beal, Buffy Krause, Kathleen Oliver, Rebecca Currie, Noni Campbell, Poesy Barlow, Jill Tremlett Large, Judy Wooten, Nancy Soward, Nancie Burton, Valerie Allis, Vicki Hamlin, Tammy Hartley, Barbara Stuvick, Amy Bland, Carolyn Akcan, Linda Patton and Mary Ellen

Box taught me what retail philanthropy is all about and made me laugh with stories about letters they receive from people like "the Virgin Mary."

During most of the time I spent traveling to do interviews and writing this book, I worked at Germanna Community College in Fredericksburg. I'd like to thank Barbara Taylor, Dr. Jeanne Wesley, Dr. Ann Woolford-Singh, Victoria Waldron, Judy Napier and Dr. David A. Sam for their belief in and support of this project. They fully understand that Doris is a national treasure.

At *The Free Lance-Star*, Josiah P. Rowe, Charles Rowe, Florence Rowe Barnick, Nick Cadwallender, Ed Jones, Jim Toler, Howard Owen, Nancy Moore, Maria Carrillo, Gwen Woolf, Cathy Jett, Eric Sundquist, Katherine Shapleigh, Paul Akers, Kevin Kirkland, Mike Allen, Brian Baer, Clint Schemmer, Amy Satterthwaite, Laura Moyer, Bill Freehling, Dave Smalley, Pam Gould, Amy Umble, Daryl Lease, Larry Evans, Ben Sellers and Lisa Chinn taught me everything I know about telling a story. So if I've failed here, they're to blame.

My late mother, Jean Oravits, was an editor, and my father, Stan Zitz, was a journalist before becoming an Army officer. They helped me enormously when I was a child by discussing national and world events with me—and listening to my own thoughts—with the same kind of respect and in much the same way that Howard Buffett did with his children, Warren, Doris and Bertie.

Most of all, I'd like to thank my wife Lisa for her love and support and belief in me. Without her, I was in a world of trouble. With her, all things are possible.

OREWORD

My sister, Doris, is a philanthropist, but far from an ordinary one. Some people write a large number of checks; others invest a large amount of time and effort. Doris does both. She's smart about how she does it as well, combining a soft heart with a hard head.

Doris wisely employs a multiplier factor in her philanthropy, getting others—an army of "Sunbeams"—to aid her. These troops don't enlist for pay, but rather are inspired by Doris' goal of helping those who have suffered bad breaks in life and have had their plight ignored by others.

If you've created your own problems, don't bother to call Doris. If some undeserved blow has upended you, however, she will spend both her money and time to get you back on your feet. Her interest in you will be both personal and enduring.

I've never believed that in philanthropy, merit should be measured by dollars expended. Lower-income individuals dropping a few dollars into a collection plate every Sunday are likely giving up something their families would enjoy—a more extensive vacation, improvements to their home or the like. Real sacrifice is involved.

To the contrary, neither I nor my children have ever foregone a purchase because the money needed for it was instead allocated to philanthropy. Our gifts, however large, have *never* impinged on our lifestyle.

Doris, by no means, lives a spartan life. But she *does* give away money that, were it used personally, would make her life easier. She is one of the rare well-off individuals who reduces her net worth annually by making charitable contributions. She thus marginally reduces her own standard of living so that she can vastly improve the quality of life for thousands of others. For Doris, a lot of good for others takes precedence over small amounts of good for herself.

More than a century ago, Andrew Carnegie wrote his famous *Gospel of Wealth*, concluding, "the man who dies rich dies disgraced." Carnegie eventually walked his talk, but only after dallying a bit. At seventy-five, he had given away less than half of his fortune, either because of a supreme optimism about his health or because he enjoyed tempting fate. (He then avoided "disgrace" for all time by making a huge gift to the Carnegie Corporation.) Doris, it should be noted, has followed Carnegie's dictum far more religiously. If she has her way, the last check she writes will be returned to the payee with "insufficient funds" stamped on it.

I don't want to close without telling you about what I believe started Doris on this path. She—and our sister, Bertie, and I—were educated by a wonderful man, our father, Howard Buffett. His love for us was unlimited and unconditional. He encouraged us to go our own way, instilling in each of us a confidence in our potential. The route Doris has taken would please our father beyond measure.

—Warren E. Buffett

To Doris — With Love — Warren

Doris hugs baby Warren in 1931.

"Let me tell you something you already know. The world ain't all sunshine and rainbows. It's a very mean and nasty place, and I don't care how tough you are, it will beat you to your knees and keep you there permanently if you let it. You, me, or nobody is gonna hit as hard as life. But it ain't about how hard you hit. It's about how hard you can *get* hit and keep on movin' forward—how much you can *take* and keep movin' forward."

—Rocky Balboa

"Our greatest glory is not in never falling, but in getting up every time we do."

—Confucius

Here's the Deal

This couldn't be right.

I was looking for a place to rent. A friend had given me an address on Sophia Street in Fredericksburg, Virginia, and said to talk to the lady there. When I pulled up to Mary Washington Square, one of the most exclusive addresses in town, I was sure my friend must've been having some fun with me.

I was a newspaper reporter, and he knew that meant I wasn't looking for a place in the high-rent district. And I was single. I needed only a one-bedroom apartment. Maybe, I thought, one of the floors was being rented out. That seemed highly unlikely. I knocked on the door. It swung open to reveal a striking gray-haired woman in her sixties with piercing blue eyes and high cheekbones.

I had no idea who she was. And I was a stranger to her.

She gave me a five-minute tour of the place. Three bedrooms. Three-and-a-half baths. Lavishly furnished with antiques. The third-floor balcony overlooked the Rappahannock River with a view of Chatham, a mansion where George Washington had spent time visiting friends, and that had been used by the Union Army during the Battle of Fredericksburg.

"Are you interested?" she said.

"I don't think I can afford this," I said.

"How much do you want to pay a month?" she asked.

I hesitated. Even then, nearly twenty years ago now, the place could probably easily bring $2,500 a month. But I figured I might as well give her an answer. "Five hundred dollars," I said, expecting her to laugh.

"Here's the deal," she said. "My husband and I will be living in North Carolina, and we'd like to come up and visit for a weekend about every six weeks. We'd like to use one of the bedrooms. Would that be OK?"

I figured I could live with that.

She didn't ask for a reference. We had known each other for minutes, hadn't talked much, but she recognized something in me.

It was 1992, and I had become one of the first of thousands of people Doris Buffett would personally size up and decide to help, one by one, most times after painstaking study, but sometimes, as in my case, on pure gut instinct.

She jokes now that we "lived together" for two years. I came to know her as a quick-witted woman with a wicked sense of humor and an infectious laugh. And as one who was mildly frustrated with her brother for his reticence at that time to let go of Berkshire Hathaway stock to help the needy. Why sell it now, Warren Buffett reasoned in the 1990s, when it would be worth so much more later and could do so much more good then?

But Doris felt a sense of urgency. Poor children needed help now, not later, she reasoned, or a whole generation could be lost to prisons and homeless shelters.

Much later, in August 2007, Sally Beatty of *The Wall Street Journal* lauded Doris for devoting her life and fortune to helping others. She has done so through her own Sunshine Lady Foundation—begun four years after we had met—and then, starting in 2007, on behalf of her brother,

Warren Buffett, then the world's richest man. He asked her to handle thousands of letters he had begun receiving from those in need around the world, after announcing he would donate about $30 billion to the Bill and Melinda Gates Foundation upon his death.

"We are really polar opposites in our approach to this," Warren said about his sister's approach to philanthropy. "I admire the way she does it more than the way I do it. She really goes at this and gets involved. I mean she really likes the retail aspect and I'm total wholesale. I can get touched by stories, but I know if I got into it, I'd get a million letters a week. It'd totally swamp everything I do. So having Doris as a partner is the perfect solution."

The Wall Street Journal said: "While it's not unheard of for people in need to write to wealthy people seeking help, philanthropy experts say it's highly unusual for a wealthy person to give so much money directly to so many individuals. Ms. Buffett's direct approach, her personal involvement and her reliance on friends and other non-professionals set her apart from other foundations, especially large, historic institutions such as the Ford Foundation, which boast staffs of trained professionals and a network of offices."

The *Journal* story noted that Doris has not always been wealthy. She had to "count pennies" as a young housewife in Colorado. She nearly lost her home in Virginia after the stock market crash of 1987. She didn't know real wealth until she inherited money from her mother in 1996. And yet, even during recent frightening economic times, rather than clinging to her money out of fear of ending up in trouble herself once more, she has continued to make giving it away to those in need her mission in life.

All of it.

"My goal," Doris likes to say with a chuckle, "is for the last check I write to bounce."

Doris and Sunshine Lady Foundation's Diane Grimsley at Beaufort-Morehead City, N.C. Airport. MICHAEL ZITZ.

Mommy Dearest

When Doris was twelve, she locked herself in a closet. "I won't remember this when I'm forty," she kept whispering to herself, crying. Outside the door, her mother, Leila Buffett, continued one of a lifelong series of tirades which would sometimes go on for two hours. "She was never happy 'til I was sobbing," Doris said.

One of Leila's favorite themes was Doris' supposed stupidity. Over and over, she would mock her by punctuating insults with "Duh!"

Leila would also make her son, Warren, cry. As a young boy, he said he often felt the urge to protect his older sister. "But I never did, because I was afraid of becoming the target myself." Once he ran away from home to escape her rants.

"Her fury would come 'in spurts,'" he said, "minute by minute. She would really lay into Doris or me. We had a mutual aid society." He chuckles about it now, downplaying it. But Warren told his first wife Susie that he was surprised Doris didn't end up in a mental institution because of the abuse.

When Warren and Doris were in their late twenties, they went to visit their father, Howard Buffett, to ask for his help in ending decades of emotional abuse by their mother. "She has to let up on us or we're moving away," they told him. Howard must've said something, because Leila toned it down for a while.

When Doris was born, on February 12, 1928, her grandparents "went nuts," she said. "They wanted to declare it a national holiday." But it was a difficult delivery for Leila, who developed an infection and almost died.

Some later believed that she developed postpartum depression. "It was a long postpartum," Doris joked. "It ended with her death." Decades later, Doris came to the conclusion that her mother may have suffered from bipolar disorder, because she would tear into her oldest daughter at the kitchen table for an hour, then smile and say pleasantly, "I'm glad we had this discussion."

Leila was a pretty, petite and vivacious woman with brown hair and green eyes. "And as my father said, she could make more friends than he could lose," Doris remembered. "It was always fun to watch her work her way across a room, because she was a born campaigner." When her husband Howard was elected to Congress, Leila worked tirelessly in his office on Capitol Hill, typing letters for no pay, "and she enjoyed that."

Leila was so well-liked that when she was sixty-five she got sixty-five birthday cards, Doris recalled. One of Doris' grandsons, Alexander Buffett Rozek, recalls Leila as a sweet great-grandmother. He treasures a picture of himself as a child standing next to Leila, who was a good enough sport in her nineties to don a dark cape and Darth Vader helmet and mask to amuse Alex, a *Star Wars* fan.

Warren doesn't believe his mother was bipolar. "There were periods she would attribute to neuralgia. I think they refer to it now as migraines. But I think my mother did have terrible headaches, and how much of these periods

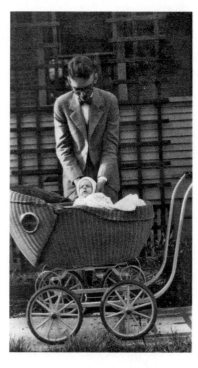

*Doris with her beloved
father, Howard.*

*Doris with her mother
Leila, outside their home
at 4224 Barker Avenue
in Omaha.*

of extreme criticism and extended berating of us would be attributable to that would be hard to tell."

He said a difficult childhood may also have contributed to it. "My mother had this tough upbringing." Leila's mother had been institutionalized for mental illness.

"Our mother always presented this totally sunny disposition to the rest of the world," Warren said. "So there was this contradiction between public and private behavior that I'm sure was hard for Doris or myself to fully understand as a kid."

But Doris said it was clear that she was the primary target of her mother's wrath. "I never heard the words, 'I love you,'" she said. "I never had a story read to me. Rarely was I tucked into bed. Nobody ever said, 'Call us when you get there so we know you're safe.' There were so many times I just wished some fairy godmother would come and understand me or like me—whisk me out of there or something."

One Christmas in Washington, in a moment of adolescent drama, a sixteen-year-old Doris angrily threw a letter from a boyfriend into the fireplace. Dried greens in the fireplace then burst into flames, flared up and scorched the mantle. Eleven-year-old Bertie decided to take the blame because she and thirteen-year-old Warren knew the punishment would be so much worse for Doris.

"We got enormous approval from my dad," Warren said. "We never could quite get it from our mother. That wasn't just Doris, that was me, too. It probably didn't extend to Bertie so much, being the youngest. Every child seeks approval from both parents. Neither Doris nor I would get much from our mother. It was tougher on her, being the oldest."

And Warren was a boy. "It was a Victorian thing," Doris said. "Your job was to make them look good, even walk a couple of steps behind them."

Leila with baby Bertie, Doris and Warren. 1934.

Younger sister Roberta Buffett Elliott of Carmel, California, agreed with Doris that Leila was much tougher on her. "Warren was a boy, and boys, in my mother's viewpoint, were more valuable than women.

"Men were supposed to be smarter. In a marriage, if the woman was smarter, she'd better hide it. Men had to go out in the world and earn the living. They had more power, and women were expected to smile and keep quiet.

"My mother never criticized my dad," Bertie said. "It's hard to imagine a marriage where you'd never feel critical, but if she did, I never saw it expressed. So I think that even though my brother was criticized, too, that it was against a background of men succeeding and being somebody and being important. My mother helped Warren by getting up early and making his breakfast so he could do paper routes. In a sense, she had higher expectations for him, so I think that would be very empowering. For a woman it was like, 'Oh, don't you dare have those expectations, because you're a woman. You can't do those things. You have to be in a lesser role.' So I think it would be more damaging to Doris than to Warren."

Leila never displayed her ill temper to Howard. She was head over heels in love with and slavishly devoted to her husband for life. When Howard, then a stockbroker, asked her, "Mom, why do you think you're here on Earth?" she replied, "To take care of you, Daddy." She really felt that way, Doris said. Leila was either J. A. Stahl's daughter, Howard Buffett's wife or Warren Buffett's mother. "That was her identity. And it really burned her up when I didn't seem to buy into that."

Leila often told Doris that she wasn't smart. She didn't want her to go to college. "She didn't see any reason. The only reason you went to college was to get your man, your 'Mrs. degree.' Ick."

Sister Bertie in her early teens.

But her younger sister Bertie was sent off to Northwestern at sixteen. Doris was never allowed to leave home to go to college, and took college classes in Washington and Omaha while her friends all went away to school.

All four of Doris' marriages were disasters. After Leila's death, Doris saw a daybook her mother had kept for decades. An entry from Doris' first marriage, when she and her husband were struggling financially, noted: "Doris called collect today."

Doris lost everything in the 1987 stock market crash, going $2 million into debt. When that happened, Leila wrote in her daybook, "Don't give Doris a cent."

She has battled depression at times in her life and gone to a psychiatrist, trying to understand why her relationship with her mother was so ugly and how that may have affected the rest of her life. "We'll never know, because at the age of three you couldn't be that bad, and that's when it started," she said. Whatever the reason, it had a huge impact on her life.

Looking at a picture of herself as a cherubic blond toddler, Doris said, "How could you hate that child? Their nickname for me was 'Mary Sunshine.'"

Doris, Bertie and Warren, in the front yard of the home the family occupied in Washington, during World War II, when Howard was in Congress.

"When I was twenty-eight and married, I remember thinking 'Isn't this strange? My brother's a genius, my sister's a Phi Beta Kappa, we all have the same parents, and I'm such a dummy.' I bought it. I really believed that." Much later, she discovered that the woman who had administered an IQ test to Bertie, Warren and Doris when they were eight, ten and twelve, respectively, was still alive. Doris checked the results: her IQ test result was 150, a couple of points lower than Warren's and a couple higher than Bertie's. "I don't know that I believed it, but I immediately joined Mensa because I could get in on that score," she said with a chuckle.

"You knew that, if you were in the family," Warren said, "there was never anyone who was smarter than the other or pulling up the rear. That was clear at the dinner table," he said. "We all had this high energy level and aspiration level. My dad thought the world of his three children; but the way the world was, boys had a different future than girls. They got out of school and wore an apron, basically. My dad wanted me to go to Wharton. I wasn't too keen on that. My guess is that he didn't much care where Doris or Bertie went. It's not that he didn't care about them. It's just that it didn't make that much difference.

"She would have been a terrific anything," Warren said. "She could've been a Johnny Carson or something like that. Fast and funny women, though, that was different from being a funny guy."

Leila's words struck Doris with such force that she hasn't ever been able to see in herself what the rest of the world sees in her. "The more important the person is to you, the more it sticks," Warren said.

Doris was gorgeous and bright, though a little bit of a late bloomer. "Doris was a total knockout and smart as anybody could be. She was a star as long as I can remember. Actually, more so than either Bertie or me. And she had a father who told her she was a star, but not a mother." Warren was two years behind her in school and he would hear stories about his older sister. "Everybody knew who Doris was. And there were plenty of boys. No shortage.

"I tell people never to use sarcasm with their kids," he said. "If you become a great actress or a billionaire, it sticks with you. She remembers the remarks from my mother more so than that every boy in the senior class wanted to go out with her. She had it all. She still does."

For years, grandson Alex said, "She felt like people in the family looked down on her because she wore her whole life on her sleeve. Everybody knew about her failed marriages. And 1987 [the mistake that wiped her out in the stock market crash] was so well-documented by the media. She felt like the black sheep of the family." It was a role her mother had prepared Doris for since she was three.

One year syndicated advice columnist Ann Landers, who was a stockholder in Berkshire Hathaway, came to an annual meeting. "What would you ask her?" someone asked Leila.

"What do you do," she replied, "when you don't like your children?"

Mother Leila with Bertie, Warren and Doris—ages 4, 6 and 9, respectively, in 1937.

A Clarion Call

"The Sunshine Lady" sat in the living room of the airy 1776 house she'd restored in downtown Fredericksburg, just across the Rappahannock River from Ferry Farm, where George Washington grew up. Sunlight streamed into the impeccably decorated room, making her blue eyes sparkle when she laughed, which she did frequently and heartily. Her hair had turned snow white, yet those eyes were not the eyes of an eighty-two-year-old, but of a seventeen-year-old, full from moment to moment of wonder, or joy, or mischief, or excitement about some new idea.

People stood on their tiptoes on the sidewalk of Caroline Street, the city's main street, straining to peer in the windows. They'd heard someone who was kind of a big deal lived there.

For fourteen years, Doris Buffett had been giving away a fortune—her own fortune—primarily to individuals "unlucky through no fault of their own." She had helped abused women become able to afford leaving destructive relationships, provided shelter and care for mentally ill people who had been living in pup tents in the woods, brought Afghan girls who wanted to go to college to America and taken them under her wing, helped elderly people who were

Doris with the college students from Afghanistan she's sponsoring at a U.S. college. Also pictured, Caroline Firestone and Molly Kelleg at Sulgrave Club in Washington.

First Lady Laura Bush asked for Doris' help in rebuilding Afghanistan.

about to lose their homes, paid for college educations for prisoners, and much more.

She often dealt with the people herself, surprising them by answering their letters and e-mails with personal phone calls. Much of her work was done one-on-one; one by one by one. As this book was published in 2010, she had given away over $100 million of her own money. She didn't want the amount she had left published, but it was a lot.

She once attended the funeral of a wealthy woman. "And all they could say about her was that she loved to shop. I thought to myself, 'I have to do better than that.'"

So she was racing against time after two transient ischemic attacks (warning strokes), to give it all away—painstakingly, carefully—in ways that would do the most good for the most people. As the word spread, she received more letters each week, and each week hard economic times made the pleas for help more desperate.

The pace was hectic even before things exploded in 2007. *The Wall Street Journal* took notice because her brother Warren Buffett added some of his own money to the towering pile for which she had to ferret out the right recipients, while beginning to pass along thousands of letters he himself was getting.

"She's always had enormous empathy for the person who has really gotten a short straw in life," Warren said. "She's not indiscriminate about who she helps and she shouldn't be. So if people keep bringing trouble on themselves, she's not going to change that. But when people have terrible experiences, and they do, unrelated to their actions, it hits a chord with her immediately."

Media coverage continued, including a feature on the *CBS Evening News* in December 2009, with Katie Couric ending her broadcast by saying, "Thank you, Doris," and that kind of exposure increased the number of cries for help.

Despite the warning strokes, she pushed ahead with the work and worried there wouldn't be enough time to do all that needed to be done; to help all who genuinely needed "a hand up, not a handout." For thousands of people who needed help, and for millions more learning how she was delivering it, she'd made "hope" more than a campaign slogan.

And yet the Sunshine Lady saw shadows lengthening over America. Despite the perky, optimistic nickname, she was far from a Pollyanna. Despite the millions she'd been giving, taking aim at problems with the precision of a sniper, she knew she could only make a tiny dent in the misery around her with her own direct actions.

She hoped media coverage of her unusual work would spur others to investigate needs in their own communities and volunteer their time, setting off a sort of ripple-effect "pay it forward" movement. An Australian mathematician calculated that if such a movement took hold in that nation, with someone doing something big for another person, and that person reaching out to three others, it would take only seventeen steps to affect the whole nation's population of twenty million.

In the film *Pay It Forward*, an inmate tells a reporter he's helped spread the word about "paying it forward" inside prison walls. It seems mawkish. And the idea that it could happen in real life is farfetched.

But life imitated art in 2009. After meeting Doris at a prison graduation ceremony, an inmate at the Auburn Correctional Facility in Auburn, New York, wrote a letter to her saying he was deeply affected by the fact that she had reached out to him and other prisoners personally, and told her he's paying it forward by spreading her mantra to other inmates that education can change their lives.

The world is a big place. Changing it is far too big a job for one woman. So she focused on trying to make a difference one person at a time: one sick child, one critically ill elderly woman about to be evicted from her home, one prisoner who wanted to learn.

Doris and Warren had both gone through a transformation in terms of social awareness since the days they sat at the dinner table and listened to their father rail against Franklin Delano Roosevelt, despairing that FDR was starting the country down the road to socialism and economic ruin with big government spending projects intended to jumpstart the economy. Their father, conservative Republican Congressman Howard Buffett, would say that the dollar would soon be worth nothing because of this spending.

Doris had been through FDR's New Deal and LBJ's Great Society and seen many lifted out of poverty, but despairs that we seem to be sliding backward.

She'd gone from being a leader of an Omaha Republican ladies' anti-communism league and working as a "Goldwater Girl" in the 1950s and '60s, to supporting Barack Obama, as her brother did, in 2008.

She'd been knocked down time and again herself by a mother who may have been bipolar, by ugly divorces, by two bouts with cancer, by strained relationships with her three children, by falling $2 million in debt—which left her sleeping on a cot, on the verge of homelessness. She'd spent days so depressed she couldn't get out of bed. And yet she kept opening her heart, giving of herself and doing it with great gusto.

But the Sunshine Lady didn't look back like a comforting grandmother and say not to worry, we've been through all this before, everything will be fine.

Even though she voted for and admires President Obama, and keeps a button from his inauguration on a side table in

U.S. Representative Howard Buffett's official 1943 congressional photograph.

her living room, she doubts that he can really change the way government does things. The rich, she said, have too much power for that. "People are bought and sold," she said of Congress. "They only tried to buy my father once. Then they gave up. But for every case we hear about, there's probably thirty more. I don't know if they're corrupt when they are voted in, or if they become corrupt when they're sworn in."

Public service is now held in such low regard that she feels she has to apologize for her father having served in Congress. "It's a terrible state of affairs. I used to be very proud of that and now I follow that by saying, 'And he was one of the few honest congressmen there.'"

Her father had wanted to be a newspaperman before going into politics. And she made the journalist's mission of "Comforting the afflicted and afflicting the comfortable" her own.

She complains about, "The bank bailouts and then the corporate bonuses—taking the country down the tubes and getting paid more to do it.

"Because Rush Limbaugh got great care, he said our health care system is in good shape. I beg to differ." Those without Limbaugh's money could not get the same kind of care, if any, she said.

In her work, Doris has heard stories like the one about a grandmother sitting on a couch saying to her five-year-old grandchild, "Get out of here!" because she was doing cocaine. "Or you ask a mother what grade her child is in and she says, 'I don't know. You'll have to ask him.' When there are [young] girls spending a week on someone's couch in a house full of adults, and then on to the next couch in another house because they have no place else to go. . . ." Before she started The Sunshine Lady Foundation in 1996,

"I didn't know there were pregnant fourteen-year-old girls living outside in tents.

"I just see a big breakdown. And you would think that rich people who have children and grandchildren might be willing to get in there and do what they can. It's an opportunity for white-haired people to do something meaningful for their children—other than leaving them money—which will probably corrupt them.

"You keep hearing this stuff and reading about it and seeing it on TV, and if you don't do anything about it, you get very depressed."

Doris believes we can't wait for change to come from a dysfunctional government—that we must change things ourselves, person by person, neighborhood by neighborhood.

When she heard that the city of Fredericksburg would have to charge admission to a new swimming pool it built near the black neighborhood of Mayfield, she saw something in that not only wrong, but illogical. The idea was to allow everyone, not just those with money, the chance to swim. As obvious as that might seem, when she started covering the admission charges every year for the Dixon Street Park Pool, she recalls a Fredericksburg socialite saying, "Pool? What do we need a pool for? We've got the country club." When the city hesitated to accept her offer to cover admission charges, she threatened to set up a card table outside the pool and hand out five-dollar bills instead.

When she heard a junior high school in Elkins, West Virginia was dilapidated and that its ceilings were full of asbestos, she took matters into her own hands.

TheInterMountain.com said:

Gone are the non-matching desks; beat-up lockers with missing bottoms that had to be shared with someone

The Dixon Street Park Pool was the first public pool in Fredericksburg. To make sure all children may enjoy it, Doris covers admission charges. When the city hesitated, she threatened to set up a card table and hand out $5 bills. REPRINTED WITH PERMISSION FROM THE FREE LANCE-STAR.

Doris as Homecoming Queen at Elkins (West Virginia) Middle School, which she renovated in 2010. Diane Grimsley.

else; and toilets left over from the 1950s. The halls and
gym are bright, almost like the sun is shining in.

She wants poor children, sick kids and abused women to experience a little happiness, even if it doesn't end up changing their lives. "I think happiness is very elusive when you're dealing with loss throughout your life. Some people are dealing with it on a daily basis. They never get away from it. Which is why I do things like camps. I just want to give them a break. What's better than some happy memories?"

But there's more to it than that. She's making sure that the people she helps make good choices, by holding them accountable, and requiring them to make good decisions. "In the back of your head somewhere you hope that maybe a miracle will occur. I'm an evangelical, and I'm waiting for the second coming."

Paying it forward requires no cash. Even those with no money to spare can make a difference in their communities. No one should use the excuse that they don't have the money to make an impact. "That's a cop-out. You can do some volunteer work in your locality." Those who do have money to give may say they don't have the time to personally find the right people to help. "There's an opportunity in the paper every day."

She believes she can make the greatest difference in the lives of young children. Studies have shown that when young children are abused, their frontal lobes, the part of the brain that deals with logic, judgment and decision-making, are affected. "I thought, 'Maybe we should be doing something at the beginning.'"

One of the first steps she took in that direction was donating $3 million to the state of Maine to build its

Educare program. She had learned about the program from Warren's daughter, Susan. "When I saw Educare, it was something I could really believe in." Experts say that eighty-five percent of brain development takes place before age three, yet only three percent of public dollars spent on education go to teaching children before they enter kindergarten. Poor children fall behind and never catch up.

The Educare model created full-day, year-long places of learning for at-risk preschoolers. Educare Central Maine is expected to open in the Fall of 2010, using the funds Doris donated, along with money from the Buffett Family Foundation, the Bill and Joan Alfond Foundation, federal stimulus funds, and local donations.

"If you can help children from infancy to age five, you can make a huge difference in the world," she said. "Brian Fischer, the Commissioner of the New York State Department of Correctional Services, told me that every man in Sing Sing had a miserable childhood.

"To me, that was a clarion call to get busy taking care of little children."

Educare groundbreaking in Maine. A $3 million grant from Doris got the preschool education program started in that state.

Howard Buffett always wanted to be a journalist, in part because of his interest in politics. The son of a grocer, he majored in journalism at the University of Nebraska. But his father Ernest prevailed upon him to become a stockbroker. He started his own investment company, and did well, steadily gaining clients even through the Depression. In 1936, after having three children, Howard and Leila decided to move out of the small bungalow they had occupied and build a bigger house.

But material things weren't important to Howard and Leila. Although they were prosperous compared to most families during the Depression, Leila continued to buy the children's shoes at a discount store rather than at Omaha's upscale Kilpatrick's department store. The family went out to eat once a week, on Sundays. Howard's meal always cost sixty-five cents and everyone else's was thirty cents.

"It was never about money at our house," Doris said. "It was about saving the country."

Howard, who was a shy man by nature, forced himself to work for years to make the connections necessary to run for Congress in 1942 as a Republican. He campaigned tirelessly, with much help from the family. But even they were surprised when he won. He served two more two-year terms before losing in 1948. Then he was returned to the House in 1950, before retiring from politics, bitterly disappointed when the party didn't nominate him to run for the U.S. Senate.

As far as Doris was concerned, an old lady was the most exciting thing about Omaha. Her name was Florence Post. She was a widow, and she lacked companionship. But she had style and culture. She became Doris' window to the outside world. "She had me hooked from the beginning," Doris said. "I thought everything she did was wonderful and important. She had this enormous influence on me because I starting picking up on all that. I was like a sponge soaking it up."

Mrs. Post asked Doris to call her Auntie. Once she made a trip to New Orleans, and brought Doris back an antique push-up brass candlestick holder—which seemed like an exquisite treasure to the girl—and a black lace shawl.

While the rest of her life was predictable, there was always Auntie Post in the background—and more culture. She convinced Leila to let Doris see the opera *Madame Butterfly*.

"There was a magic about her," Doris said. "I think we filled each other's need. She spent hours making clothes for a doll Bertie had. She was just a remarkable addition to my life. She had books in her living room about antebellum houses."

Auntie Post stood in stark contrast to the rest of Doris' existence. "We walked to school and we walked home to eat our lunch. I'd have to think long and hard about what

Doris at age 17, wearing a lace shawl given to her by Auntie Post.

we talked about at the table or what we did. It was a Midwestern Depression life. Pretty simple. My family didn't drink. There was no night life going on."

Doris didn't mind looking out for little brother Warren, whom she said was never any trouble. At a young age, it became clear that Warren had a gift for math inherited from Leila, who had been an outstanding math student at the University of Nebraska, but had dropped out to marry Howard. "He could tell you all the batting averages. He loved numbers."

Soon he started to focus on ways to make money. At age six he went door to door selling chewing gum. "He sold Cokes and made a nickel for every carton of six," Doris said. He wore a nickel-plated coin changer on his belt that he had been given for Christmas. He kept moving from one enterprise to another, and by the time he was thirteen, he filed his first tax return, deducting the cost of his bike and his watch. He was continually excited about new and bigger money-making schemes. By college, he owned a gas station. As Warren was piling up cash, Doris collected autographed pictures of movie stars, and dreamed of escaping Omaha and her mother.

As she became a beautiful young woman, her mother's attacks increased in intensity. Once, when they drove from Omaha to Chicago, Leila raged at Doris nonstop all the way across Iowa. As time passed, "The main thing was to stay out of trouble," Doris said. She'd go through stretches in which she didn't date, babysitting instead to avoid her mother's fury.

At the time, she would never have dreamed her mother might be jealous. Her self-esteem was nonexistent. "I was supposed to be so good looking; but I'll tell you when I was teen-age to college age, I could tell you every detail that was wrong from the tip of my head to the tip of my very large feet. Because of things my mother said, I never saw myself as pretty. It stays with you. It's an imprint on your little juvenile brain."

Years later, she went to a psychiatrist to try to deal with the damage done by the emotional abuse, and to understand why her mother behaved that way. "The shrink and I were trying to figure it out and that's what we came up with: I think there was a lot of envy and jealousy when I was a teenager—that's typical." Doris was young and pretty and having a good time. Leila's youth had been anything but glamorous. Her own mother, Stella Stahl, was mentally ill and abusive. Leila had been working nonstop since childhood.

Despite her devotion to Howard, Leila's own story must have seemed like a twisted sequel to "Cinderella." Instead of living happily ever after with her prince, she merely traded one form of bondage for another, the drudgery of her life continuing while her carefree daughter was off to the ball, laughing merrily.

Leila and Howard had never been accepted by the upper-class kids in their youth, Bertie said. Then she watched as her oldest daughter was not only pursued by boys, but embraced by the in-crowd. "My parents weren't social climbers," Bertie said. And Leila saw Doris as not only a social climber, but the same kind of girl who had snubbed her in high school. When Doris saved her babysitting money to buy fashionable clothes, it made her mother even more resentful.

Because of her mother's illness, Leila had to take on some of her responsibilities in the home at the age of five. Then, when her father bought a newspaper business so he could work at home and watch the kids, she had to set type and run a loud Linotype press. The noise caused Leila to

BACK ROW (LEFT TO RIGHT) — THE BUFFETT SIBLINGS: *Clarence,*
Mrs. Burkholder, the housekeeper, George, Howard, Alice, Fred,
Grandpa Ernest. FRONT ROW (LEFT TO RIGHT) — THE SPOUSES:
Helen with baby Barbara, Warren, baby Bertie on Leila's lap, Doris,
Katie with Billy on her lap, George, Bob on Irma's lap. 1934.

have headaches and miss school. She was gifted at math, a trait she passed on to Warren, but dropped out of school at the University of Nebraska to marry Howard.

"My life was so easy compared to what hers had been," Doris said. "I didn't have to put out a newspaper. And she never had a date until she met my father."

But acknowledging the fact that Leila's life had been hard doesn't undo the damage. She even made Warren cry. Finally, "I ran away," he said. His mother's fits of rage drove him out onto the streets of Washington at age thirteen. Police found him and brought him home the next day.

Although Leila didn't behave that way in front of Howard, he clearly knew something was wrong, because he would warn the children when he sensed an attack coming on: "Watch out, Mom's on the warpath." Apparently he wasn't aware of how extreme the outbursts were. So he never intervened. But Leila never crushed Doris' spirit to the point where she lost her curiosity about the world.

In Washington, Bertie was old enough for Doris to start passing on what she had learned from Auntie Post. "One of the things that she added to my life was that she was more interested in cultural things," Bertie said. They went to see *Mr. Roberts* together in Washington, and to the musical *Carousel*. "That wouldn't have happened except for her interests," Bertie said. "Those things are highlights in my life. The arts became very important. It's one of my passions. She had a curiosity and desire to know about some of these things that I benefited from. It enriched my life. My dad was busy with his work, and Warren was busy learning how to make more and more money. And my mother was just sort of stuck in her everyday life. Doris was the person who provided me with adventure."

Christmas Day photo from 1938. Warren with his coin changer, Doris and Bertie with dolls, all looking miserable outside their home in Omaha.

Reenactment of 1938 Christmas photo at Bertie's birthday party in Carmel, California in 2006.

Mr. Buffett Goes to Washington

Howard Buffett's election to Congress in 1942 led to an unexpected change in Doris' life. "We left Omaha, where life was totally predictable—day by day, year by year—to move to Washington, a completely different culture."

In January of 1943, the Buffett family boarded a train to Washington, carrying baskets of food Grandpa Ernest Buffett had packed for them. There were thousands of Marines on the train returning to their base in Quantico.

Grandpa had seen to it that the family had a private room on the train so no one would catch diseases from these soldiers returning from the Pacific. "That was his great fear," Doris said.

They received house-hunting advice from Frank and Marian Reichel, whom Howard had met when he was a stockbroker. The Reichels lived in Fredericksburg, and said Washington was simply a horrible place to raise a family. On their advice, Howard rented the Payne house across the Chatham Bridge from Fredericksburg. It was an hour's drive from the U.S. Capitol building, long before Interstate 95 and Beltway gridlock.

Frank Reichel had founded the Sylvania plant near Fredericksburg in 1929, and made a fortune producing cellophane. When Sylvania merged with American Viscose, he became president and chairman of the board of both companies. It turned out the Reichels had ulterior motives in steering the Buffetts away from Washington. Marian wanted to make a match between Doris and their son Frank Jr. By age fourteen, Doris was already a model-like five-foot-six, taller than most other girls. "How tall is he?" Doris asked after the move to Fredericksburg. "Tall enough," Marian replied. Marian expressed the hope that Doris and her son would marry, often telling her coyly, "and I have this six-carat diamond for his bride." Marian was disappointed when Doris and Frank Jr. never got together. Even though he was good-looking, there was simply no chemistry between them.

The Payne house sat atop a hill overlooking the Rappahannock River and the town. The house, which had a swing on the front porch, formal gardens, a cutting garden, a greenhouse and ten fireplaces, was palatial compared to the Buffett home in Omaha. It was a stately home with a breathtaking view, surrounded by history and architecture that fascinated Doris. It looked down on a town architecturally preserved from colonial times and Civil War days. There were trenches in the front yard of the Payne house that Union troops had dug during the Battle of Fredericksburg in 1862.

It was actually across the Rappahannock, not the Potomac River, where folklore has it that young George Washington threw the silver dollar. It's believed that George may well have thrown a flat, round coin-sized stone—not a silver dollar, which wouldn't have existed when Washington was a young man—across the Rappahannock at a point just below the Buffetts' new home. It's narrow enough there for that to be possible for someone with a strong throwing arm.

The greatest baseball pitcher of all time couldn't come close to throwing a rock across the Potomac.

The Buffetts' house wasn't far from Ferry Farm, where Washington grew up. Ferry Farm is the site of the legend of his chopping down the cherry tree, a complete fabrication, but good for selling history textbooks in the nineteenth century and good for tourism today. And the Buffetts were next door to Chatham, which had served as a headquarters for the Union army during the Civil War.

"I'd never seen a lovelier place," Doris said. "I had tears in my eyes. It was everything I'd ever dreamed of. That was heaven for me." She always had an innate talent for decorating. "I remember at the age of six thinking, 'I don't like that door.' Nobody told me anything about it. I had an eye for decorating, and for color as well. That was why I loved the Payne house."

If it was heaven for Doris, it was hell for Leila. "It terrified her," Doris said. Leila, understandably, never wanted to leave Nebraska. "My mother was a small-town girl from Nebraska and liked things the way they were," she said.

Warren agreed: "She left all of her friends behind when she moved to Washington—she didn't enjoy political life. She didn't talk about this because she wouldn't do anything that would knock my dad; but she was making sacrifices, and pretty big ones, in terms of the life she enjoyed living because of what my dad did. She never complained about it, but that doesn't mean it wasn't affecting her inside."

The day after they arrived, a neighbor picked the Buffett children up and took them to school and, as far as Doris was concerned, things just kept getting better. "I loved James Monroe High School," she said. "You could get away with anything. You could run to the window when a plane passed over. It was just a cinch."

Doris turned fifteen a few weeks after moving to Fredericksburg. Her good looks and obvious excitement about the place instantly made her one of the most popular girls in town. The cool kids in Fredericksburg were impressed with her, and she with them. "I thought they dressed so well. They were the epitome of style, I thought. Coming from the Midwest I was just star struck when I got here."

Meanwhile, twelve-year-old Warren was desperately homesick. He claimed to be allergic to something in this strange new place. "My brother said he couldn't breathe in his bedroom, couldn't sleep, and that he stood up in his bed all night." He wrote one letter after another to Grandpa Buffett, saying he was ill and begging to come live with him. "It got him a ticket back home to Omaha," she said. "This was his way to go back."

Nine-year-old Bertie also wanted to go home, but the same trick didn't work twice with Grandpa Buffett. "Bertie spent the whole time moping," Doris said. "She rarely went to school. She just plain didn't want to be here and she pouted most of the time. I had the time of my life, and I loved the town. I loved the architecture. And everybody was so nice. I felt that charm was invented in Fredericksburg. In Omaha, everything was sturdy, would last for 400 years, but there was no charm. In Fredericksburg, things might have been held up with thumbtacks, but the charm was there."

Bertie explained: "I probably was mad, but mostly I was lonely—leaving my friends and my grandpa Buffett and my cousin, Bill Buffett, and my neighborhood friends. It was a different culture. The South was different than Omaha then. There were still segregated schools. I had trouble understanding some Southern accents. We lived in a house that was very beautiful, up on a hill, but there were no neighborhood kids. It did teach me something wonderful though. We had a nice middle-class house in Omaha. We moved to this house in Fredericksburg, which to me was something out of the movies—a very romantic place—and really pretty, and so I learned at an early age that living in a beautiful house isn't the secret to happiness. Doris had a wonderful time. She was the belle of the ball. Her friends had cars. It was wonderful for her. In Fredericksburg, she was with the 'in' group of kids. In Omaha she wasn't because she wasn't going to the right school."

Fredericksburg was established in 1728 as a port for Spotsylvania County. The colonial town's streets were named for members of the royal family. The downtown house Doris herself would buy and restore later is embedded with a cannon ball from the Civil War.

Chatham also served as a field hospital during the Civil War. Clara Barton and poet Walt Whitman tended to the wounded troops there. George Washington visited Chatham in colonial times, and Abraham Lincoln stopped there during the Civil War. Young Doris was convinced that ghosts from the Civil War were her next-door neighbors. She was standing in a gazebo with friends, taking pictures of Chatham, and she thought she saw a shade move in the mansion, which was known to be unoccupied. "That terrified me," she said.

It turned out that John and Lillian Pratt, the owners, who were in the process of restoring Chatham, spent the winter in warmer climes because oil rationing made it difficult to heat the mansion. The Pratts became good friends with the Buffetts. John Lee Pratt, a native of neighboring King George County, was on the board of General Motors. Secretary of State George Marshall came to Chatham as the Pratts' guest to go duck hunting.

"I think Mr. Pratt and my father had the same views on politics," Doris said. They heard the ghost story and played along, with Lillian Pratt telling Doris sternly that *no one* was allowed to take pictures of Chatham. "And I had a picture-book full," Doris said. "I was scared. I thought I was going to have to destroy the pictures and burn the negatives. Mrs. Pratt was scary. She was very stuffy. She had a complete set of diamonds, sapphires and rubies. On the Fourth of July, she showed up at an event wearing a string of big pearls with a gigantic one dangling as a pendant. That was summer casual for her." But she did Doris a big favor.

"They invited us to come over and visit Chatham, and it was the highlight of my life—up to that point. They had a gold platter that [Russia's] Catherine the Great had given someone as a gift. And there were Fabergé eggs. My father was pretty awed by these people, and who wouldn't be? We'd never seen anything like that in Omaha. We were a simple family."

Later, the "Lillian Pratt collection" of Fabergé and other priceless Russian artifacts would become a permanent exhibit at the Virginia Museum of Fine Arts in Richmond. Ironically, the Pratts were the most notable philanthropists in Fredericksburg history until Doris returned half a century later. They would probably be categorized as "wholesale" philanthropists, but did some of the same things she does, such as giving local young people scholarships. When Pratt died in 1975, *Forbes* magazine said he was the single biggest stockholder in GM, holding 17.4 percent of its shares. His estate was divided among the University of Virginia, Johns Hopkins and Virginia Tech, and he donated Chatham to the National Park Service.

It was the history and beauty of Fredericksburg, not the wealth of its upper crust that impressed Doris the most.

Her boyfriend, David Brown, had an aunt who portrayed George Washington's mother at the Mary Washington House. She arranged for Doris to give tours of Kenmore, home of George Washington's sister, Betty. "I fell in love with it. I had an overwhelming love for American history and I responded to architecture."

Howard had been renting a small apartment in Washington during the week to reduce his commuting because of gas rationing. Leila was so determined to get out of Fredericksburg that she spent much of her time house-hunting in Washington. Her frequent absences made Doris' time there even happier.

When Leila finally found another place, Doris was sorry to leave Fredericksburg, but returned to visit often, and ultimately made it her home years later. "I would have loved to stay here. But one didn't have those choices. Although I will say Washington was very appealing. There was a lot of excitement going on."

Doris on a date, shown with Sam Fordyce's father's car, "the fastest in town."

Doris with Yves Martin, Free French Naval Ensign, at the French
Embassy birthday party for Margaret Truman.

Doris at a United States Naval Academy Ring Dance with Merrill Norton in 1947.

Doris in Annapolis, Md. with her date, Midshipman Merrill Norton in 1948.

The Buffetts moved into a two-story white colonial in Spring Valley, off Massachusetts Avenue. Doris quickly made friends at Woodrow Wilson High School.

"My father and Judge Jasper Bell, a congressman who was a Jeffersonian Democrat from Missouri, hit it off," Doris said. "Representative Bell and his wife Grace were really a darling couple. He was the first congressman I'd known who was not elderly from my point of view—probably forty-five. He and his wife were really in love and had a sense of humor." Doris liked the fact that their daughters, Betty, Beverly and Virginia, could be irreverent with their mother. When their mother was telling them what to do, they would say "Heil Hitler!" clicking their heels with a Nazi salute. "They got away with a lot more than us, but they were fun."

Doris' four years of high school coincided with World War II. "I was thrust, willingly, into a far more exciting and interesting existence than ever could have been predicted. It was a fascinating adventure for a teenage girl—especially one whose father was in Congress. I soon caught on to what made Washington tick—not money, but political power. It was pretty heady stuff. I found out that if I was pulled over for driving too fast, the policeman wouldn't give me a ticket. Wow. Just a gentle warning, after he'd checked our congressional license plate."

Because it was wartime, Washington was teeming with "dollar-a-year" people who selflessly left their jobs and homes to help with the war effort. Her high school may have had the highest enrollment of kids who were children of dollar-a-year men. The children of numerous generals and high government officials also attended Woodrow Wilson. They were a very bright group and, coming from such diverse backgrounds, far different from the provincial crowd Doris was used to.

She wasn't pressured to get good grades—beyond her parents telling her to do her best—but she did well, ranking in the top ten percent of her class. Doris jokes that she majored in clothes, boys, and her sorority, and trips on weekends to Yale, Annapolis, Harvard and West Point. "I wasn't thinking much about the future—any further, that is, than the next election. She didn't want to go back to Nebraska, which she considered "dullsville."

Doris had one very special girlfriend, Vivian Oviatt, who rode the same bus to school: "Red hair, a huge amount of fun, and crazy." They were joined on the bus by a neighbor friend, George Grizzard, who later became an actor. He was best known for his roles as an underhanded U.S. senator in the 1962 film *Advise and Consent*, as President John Adams in the PBS series *The Adams Chronicles*, and for winning an Emmy in 1980 for *The Oldest Living Graduate*. He also won a 1996 Tony Award for Best Actor for *A Delicate Balance*. Throughout high school, the three of them, Doris said, "did a huge amount of laughing."

Doris had lots of suitors, but remained "chaste," she said. "I was living in fear of my life. In high school at that time, everything depended on a girl's reputation. You would never do anything to spoil it. I feel like I'm talking about a foreign land, 300 years ago. Sixteen and never been kissed, that was me." The kissing part was soon to change, but necking was as far as things went.

"We all knew a girl at Woodrow Wilson who had a bad reputation. We didn't want to be like Trixie. There was plenty of kissing, but boys knew that 'no' meant 'no.' I was determined not to shame my family." Date rape, she said, was unheard of at that time, or at least never spoken of.

Doris was allowed to travel alone to weekend dances called "hops," and she was absolutely without fear as she tore around Washington by bus, streetcar or automobile. Looking back, she's grateful that none of her friends worried about bad things happening, allowing them to fully enjoy their limited freedom. Courtship was slow and unforced, and girls felt relatively little pressure to have sex.

"I remember going to a party where I met a bunch of handsome, quite dashing, new nineteen-year-old second lieutenants on their way to the European front as platoon commanders. It was a terrible responsibility for kids. I can't help contrasting World War II to this current horror. Then, every person in the United States was involved in some way in the war effort, whether it was a family with a son, father or brother in the military, or the way we collected scrap metal, got by on one pair of shoes a year, and never used the car unnecessarily, to save gas. We were all in it, and there was a wonderful sense of community and of unity of purpose."

She turned seventeen in 1945, the year she graduated from high school and the year the war ended. Like every girl her age, Doris had fretted over pimples and slow bust development, struggled to learn the latest dance steps, and had crushes on boys who were involved with someone else. "I finally landed a football player when I was seventeen," she said. Also typical of a teenage girl: "I was annoyed by my kid brother, embarrassed by naïve and corny parents, and humiliated by not having a date after our ritual sorority meetings on Friday nights."

Doris had become the family decorator. She chose paint colors and came up with many small projects to decorate the house. When the war ended that year, gas was available for her to drive into the countryside and hunt for antiques, which were very inexpensive then.

She was invited to a White House birthday party for Margaret Truman, the president's daughter, who was several years older than Doris. And one of her boyfriends had a connection that benefited Warren. "One thing I'll say about Doris, I usually liked her boyfriends," Warren said. "She had good taste. I can't recall any that I didn't like. She had plenty of them, of course." A boyfriend Warren particularly liked was Dudley DeGroot Jr., whose father, Dudley Sr., was the head coach of the Washington Redskins. Because of that relationship, fourteen-year-old Warren, who was a big fan, became a water boy for the Redskins for part of the 1944–45 season, when the team won the Eastern Division title.

"What I did was make myself a real pest," Warren said. "Everyone in Washington was totally Redskins nuts— including me. And Sammy Baugh was the hero of the western world. I was such a pain in the neck that Dudley, to avoid me being the little brother that was always causing trouble, made me a water boy. I wasn't the water boy that went out to the field. But I did get to be on the sidelines. I had this huge Redskins sweatshirt that fell over my shoulders—designed for a guy about three times as far across as I was."

With her father in Congress, Doris was in a privileged position that extended beyond getting out of speeding tickets. He invited intellectuals to dinner, and those evenings were eye-opening for Doris. "The conversations were all the way above those in Nebraska," she said.

Meanwhile, she, Warren and Bertie were drifting apart. In Washington, they were living lives that didn't intersect much. "Once in a while, we'd be sitting in the back seat of a car driving from Washington back to Omaha." Still, Warren and Bertie continued to try to shield Doris from Leila's wrath. "They saved my neck a couple of times. When I really would have been in trouble, they covered for me."

For one year she attended Mount Vernon Junior College in D.C., which was right around the corner from home. Then she transferred to George Washington University, because her parents didn't want her to leave home to go to school. They had no qualms about Warren leaving. In 1947, Warren enrolled at the Wharton School of the University of Pennsylvania, as his father had planned for years. Leila and Howard kept asking Doris what her major would be. She couldn't tell them, so she dropped out during her junior year at GW. She was adrift.

When Mary McNamara, an Omaha high school principal who Doris describes as four-foot-ten and ferocious, asked her what she was doing, Doris replied sheepishly that she was selling clothes at Kilpatrick's department store, along with some of her friends.

"You haven't finished college, have you?" the tough little woman asked.

"No," Doris admitted.

McNamara then uttered the words Doris would never forget: "Well, even if you do get married, there's always death, disease and divorce." Those words were to come back to haunt her more than once.

PAYING IT FORWARD

⟨ong before the making of the 2000 film *Pay it Forward*, in which a twelve-year-old boy was determined to start a movement to change the world, one person at a time, Josephine Travis understood the ripple effect an act of kindness can have.

The boy in the movie, who has an abusive father, comes up with an idea to change the world, one person at a time, with each person helped, in turn, reaching out to others. The character, played by Haley Joel Osment, explains both why the concept is necessary and why it's difficult to make it work: "I guess it's hard for people who are so used to things the way they are—even if they're bad—to change. 'Cause they kind of give up. And when they do, everybody kind of loses."

As she helps others, Doris has seen her efforts take root, bear fruit and spread. Many of those she has helped have not only thrived, but also gone into careers like nursing and working for nonprofit organizations with the intention of paying it forward.

Josephine Travis came into Doris' life when she was a newlywed who had recently moved to Colorado with her first husband, Truman Wood. She was trying to "live graciously" on $270 a month and entertain the wives of men who could help Truman's career. "I was the typical bride," polishing the silver, learning how to cook, planning dinner parties and teas. Doris was absolutely mystified as to how to get all the food she was preparing for the parties ready at the same time.

Her mother's words replayed in her head like a needle stuck on a vinyl record: *She was stupid. She would never achieve anything worthwhile. She had lost her looks when she was eighteen. She was lucky to find a man who would marry her.* It seemed to Doris that her mother must be right. Being a "good wife" and homemaker was beyond her, she thought. So she was already a failure in her own mind when she was just reaching adulthood.

Plus, Truman's career in advertising was not going well. He was becoming increasingly depressed, and Doris felt pressured to impress people in order to help him.

So she was trying desperately to fit into the mold of the dutiful, perfect 1950s "Ozzie and Harriet" housewife—a role she was ill-suited for, partly because she was far too intelligent and ambitious to settle for that, even though she didn't see herself that way.

"I was twenty-three, and Josephine was about sixty—in the prime of life, as I see it now," she said. She patiently transformed Doris into the perfect hostess.

"She was darling to me—generous and loving when I desperately needed her help with what seemed to me at the time to be a major crisis."

Doris said to her, "What can I do for you?"

"Nothing at all," Josephine said. "But someday, when you're able, help someone else."

Josephine couldn't have known she had planted the seed for the Sunshine Lady Foundation. As silly as it may sound today, hosting a tea party without a hitch was, for Doris, a step toward establishing her sense of self-worth.

A few years later, a larger step was to come in the form of an opportunity to pay it forward. Doris had joined a Denver Kappa Kappa Gamma alumni group during the winter of 1951–52 in an effort to make friends. An acquaintance from Omaha also joined. They quickly found that if you hadn't attended a Colorado school, you ended up in the kitchen, doing dishes. So they received permission to form their own newcomers' chapter along with Patty Knupp, a vivacious, bright young woman with a master's degree in geology from the University of Kansas. She had two cute little girls and drove a convertible roadster.

Patty moved to Hawaii and had a third daughter in 1955. Both mother and child developed polio the day after the baby was born. The virus didn't invade the child's central nervous system, and she recovered. But Patty, whose immune system was weakened by childbirth, was completely paralyzed. Her prognosis was poor. But she was just determined to live for her daughters, and she did.

A mercy flight took Patty from Hawaii to St. Joseph's Hospital in Omaha, which was well-known for its polio ward. When Doris went to visit, she braced herself. She found Patty in an iron lung. "An iron lung was a really scary thing in those days," Doris said. "When we were growing up, that was the scariest thing that could happen to you. But she had the same perky, indomitable spirit she had before in Denver."

Doris and her friend, Mary Rice, moved back to Omaha when their husbands were transferred there. There they "made a vow in blood" with Patty that if she kept fighting, they would be there for her. "We were going to stick it out. She never said 'Poor me,' or even looked like she felt sorry for herself."

The hospital continually put her in a room with the worst polio cases. "They would die and she would live," Doris said. Meanwhile, Patty's children were staying with her parents. Patty improved enough to get out of the iron lung and use a Monaghan lung, a smaller, portable device, to aid breathing. Then she suffered a relapse and returned to the iron lung. Doris and Mary decided to bring Patty's daughters to visit. They knew she would make a super-human effort to get out of the iron lung because she didn't want to scare the girls. She left the hospital with the Monaghan lung to go on a picnic with her daughters. "She could frog-breathe for four minutes, but if anything happened to the generator, we were in real trouble. The girls had a good time, and they didn't see their mother encased in this thing."

Patty's condition improved over an eighteen-month period at the Omaha hospital. She was a formidable bridge player, so Doris organized groups, sometimes including Warren, to come to the hospital and play with her.

Patty's husband was having a hard time adjusting. When she was sent home to Newton, Kansas, Doris visited. She found Patty in a room with no air-conditioning in the stifling Kansas summertime, bedridden, with a little window she couldn't see out of.

They launched a Kappa Kappa Gamma fundraising campaign, and added curtains and furniture. Some years later, Doris visited again and realized the roof of the family's tract home was leaking, ruining the computer Patty used by manipulating a stick she held between her teeth.

Doris wrote Warren: "You remember Patty. I know you don't give to individuals, but this is somebody you know, a real heroine. Maybe you'd like to help."

Warren responded with a letter that began with his standard answer: No, he didn't do that. Doris' heart sank.

But in the last paragraph, in a complete turnaround, he wrote: "I have set up a small foundation called The Sherwood Foundation because my children are often asked to give money. The kids wanted to call it the Robin Hood Foundation. You can give away $50,000 this year and $100,000 next year." Doris was ecstatic. "I think I probably have the only letter in which he ever said, 'I've rethought my position.'"

It was a first for Warren, too—his initial glimpse of what was to come from Doris. Beginning with Patty's situation, he gradually came to understand her mission in life. He's gained increasing respect for the surgical effectiveness of her highly personal "retail" approach to philanthropy.

Doris used the first year's money to fix the roof, install air-conditioning, and put in a large picture window. "Patty dictated a letter to me saying she was the luckiest girl in the world." Doris said. "To me she was the bravest woman in the world. And I'll never forget that. It was an earthshaking experience to be able to help someone like that."

Doctors predicted Patty would live for five years. She hung on for twenty, long enough to see her daughters grow up. She passed away in 1975, but played a major role in changing the course of Doris' life, and indirectly, those of thousands of others The Sunshine Lady Foundation would help.

Josephine Travis had asked Doris to pay it forward. In helping Patty she had, and the experience was more rewarding than she could have ever imagined.

The Sunshine Lady Foundation was founded in 1996, when Doris inherited some of her mother's Berkshire Hathaway stock. Doris had already been planning ways to use that stock, which was booming, to help others. The Foundation's name was derived from her childhood nickname, "Mary Sunshine." She had initially planned to donate money to needy and deserving individuals anonymously, simply as "the Sunshine Lady"; but when she was standing in line to open a checking account under that name, she had second thoughts. She feared that people who received anonymous checks from "the Sunshine Lady" might think it a cruel joke.

She enlisted the help of about a hundred family, friends, friends of friends and professional colleagues—technically known as "adjunct program managers"—but whom she affectionately decided to call "Sunbeams." Sunbeams alert the Foundation to needs and opportunities in their communities. They are the Sunshine Lady Foundation's radar.

In addition to recruiting Sunbeams, Doris assembled a staff that works diligently and, just as importantly, enjoys what it does. Her foundation has given away $100 million of Doris' personal fortune as of this book's publication in 2010, when she had just turned eighty-two; but she believes she still has plenty of work left to do in what might be a short time.

She's proud that the Foundation's overhead is below six percent, far less than most charitable organizations. That's possible in part because SLF doesn't have to pay someone to raise money. It all comes from Doris. Nor does it have to pay someone to invest that money. Warren does that quite well. For years, money was coming in faster than Doris could give it away as Berkshire Hathaway stock soared from $30,000 a share to $140,000. When the stock market tumbled in the fall of 2008, that trend came to an end, at least temporarily, although the stock had climbed back up to $99,000 a share by the beginning of 2010. Doris pays $400 a month to rent modest Foundation offices in Morehead City and Wilmington, North Carolina.

In 1998, she started the Peace Awards. She had long felt strongly that workers in the field of domestic violence, usually earning low wages and receiving no recognition, deserved to be honored. Every other year since 1998, she has solicited nominations for the awards, which recognize outstanding service in the field of domestic violence. Doris flies the recipients to Wilmington, shows them the town, and celebrates their contributions with a gala dinner and $10,000 checks for their personal use, no strings attached. The banquet room vibrates with mutual appreciation, joy and love.

Doris' own experience with emotional abuse led her to help battered women escape destructive homes. "As I became educated about domestic violence, I learned of the many survivors who were eager, indeed desperate, to attend college to improve their lives, and provide an independent living for themselves and their children," Doris said. To meet this need, the Foundation set up the Women's Independent Scholarship Program (WISP). Applications continue to pour into the North Carolina office from every state in the union and the Virgin Islands.

"The women are incredibly motivated," Doris said. "They do amazingly well." More than 40 percent of them maintain a grade point average of 3.5 or higher. Their children are growing up in violence-free homes. There's a photo wall in the North Carolina office with hundreds of smiling faces and bushel baskets of letters telling us how their lives have changed, and how for the first time they have hope. "As Dr. Phil would say, 'That's our payoff,'" Doris said.

"These women believe they are trapped, that they are worthless, and that they can't accomplish anything," she said. But the WISP success stories include former battered women who've gone on to many colleges, including the prestigious Wharton School of Business at the University of Pennsylvania.

Of course, much of the work of the Sunshine Lady Foundation involves weeding out requests that are unworthy.

"While we don't claim to be rocket scientists, we're diligent, we're thorough and we *are* empowering people to change their lives," Doris said. "The money available to me to fund the Sunshine Lady Foundation was made through sound investments. I, in turn, look at every grant as an investment, and a successful one at that."

Doris likes to tell the story of the woman who wrote to ask for help because she had run up $80,000 in credit card debt. She said her husband, who was an attorney making $250,000 a year, would leave her if he found out. Doris called her and suggested she get a job to pay off the debt. "But that would mean the kids would miss soccer practice," the woman said. Helping that woman wouldn't have been paying it forward, it would have been throwing money away. And, Doris said, "Wasting money is not in the Buffett DNA."

The Foundation follows two primary rules:

First, it never invests in anything Doris and her staff don't understand. That's something gleaned from Warren's approach to investing. "We are put off by buzz words, fanciful speculation, and grandiosity in general," she said. "We want plain talk."

Second, it requires collaboration in every grant it makes, large or small. "A grant without collaboration is a handout, and we never give a handout. We give a hand up. In business this is called making a deal, and we think of it the same way: we're making deals. Each recipient becomes our partner in the deal. We treat our partners with dignity and respect, and our joy comes from seeing them empowered by their own actions."

Doris hopes her experience will move others to find a way to make a positive difference in the life of another. "It seems to me that extending a hand to another person who needs help is one of the best opportunities life has to offer."

As James Barrie, the author who created Peter Pan, said, "Those who bring sunshine to the lives of others cannot keep it from themselves."

Josephine Travis knew that a long time ago.

DOING HER DUTY

$\mathcal{I}$n 1948, Republican Thomas E. Dewey was considered a cinch to win the presidency. Polls showed that Harry S Truman was an unpopular president. Worse yet, his Democratic Party had splintered into three parts. Of course, Truman pulled off the greatest upset in U.S. political history. One of the most iconic news photographs ever taken shows Truman beaming and holding up a copy of *The Chicago Tribune* with the headline, "DEWEY DEFEATS TRUMAN."

Thing was, although not many Americans were crazy about Harry, they weren't doing back flips over Dewey, either. Still, Republicans expected a rout. Dewey's lackluster appeal and the expectation of an easy victory depressed Republican voter turnout in Howard Buffett's Second Congressional District, and he lost his bid for reelection. In the long run, the defeat was more of a blow to Doris than to her father, who returned to Congress two years later.

The family went home to Omaha during one of Nebraska's worst winters. There were so many storms and so much snow that planes dropped food to cows stuck in the fields— and they still died. The house was frozen. People had difficulty getting in and out of town. Doris' friends were still

Doris, age 22, in Ak-Sar-Ben debutant ball gown in 1950. (Ak-Sar-Ben is Nebraska spelled backwards.)

away at college. She could not have felt more isolated if she had been dropped into a crater on the dark side of the moon.

Howard returned to his investment business, where his partners had taken over his clients. "But he was patient and never complained about it," Doris said. "I know it was a really hard time for him, starting over." Personally, she felt she was in a place where she couldn't start over: "I had good times in Washington, but there was no going back there. This is where I was. Warren was at the University of Nebraska main campus in Lincoln. My sister went away to Northwestern, so now all the heat was on me. I really had to get married. I looked around and there really wasn't a lot available in Omaha.

"Everybody I ever knew went away to school," she said. "Even if you just went to Lincoln—to the university—you went away. But no one went to Omaha U." That's what she called the University of Nebraska's satellite campus at Omaha. It was a single building—not much of a collegiate setting. "I took the bus there every day. That fit into my feelings about myself that I was sort of third rate."

She desperately wanted to go to Southern Methodist University after hearing about it from a friend, but her mother nixed that. Bertie said she believes that Doris' tendency to test boundaries, her love of adventure and her good looks combined to make Leila determined not to let her go away to school. Bertie said she was allowed to go away to Northwestern University near Chicago when she was only sixteen because, "I tried to be 'good' and not test those boundaries. With my nature, it wasn't hard for me to do that. As my life progressed, I've been a person who enjoys being on boards of nonprofits—I like working with other people. I've had positions of leadership, and I can do that, but I enjoy being part of a team. Both Warren and Doris have star quality. They love being the star, and they're good at it. For me, if I were in a jazz band, I'd rather be playing as one of the instrumentalists rather than the lead singer. Warren and Doris would be the lead singer. In fact, Warren's life *is* being the lead singer. I think it's just a different nature."

Doris then had a fanciful idea of going to New York City and doing some kind of work. That was also vetoed. Meanwhile, her friends were all getting engaged. She had a scrapbook stuffed with wedding notices.

She went to work selling clothes at Kilpatrick's, a department store. It was the spring of 1949, and one of the young women she worked with dressed as the Easter Bunny so mothers would bring their children to the store for photos. Truman Wood came down to see what was going on. All the girls had known each other since the eighth grade, and they all knew Truman. He had moved to Omaha after Doris left for Washington. "I'd heard about him, but never met him. I thought he was good-looking," she said. "He was somebody I could date." Doris was twenty-one.

"Now, you have to understand that couples were falling like leaves on a tree. It was marriage time in Omaha, Nebraska, and that's what you were to do—get married—the sooner, the better. There was no other course of life that was worth living at that point," she said. "In that age group, you got married. I remember five girls who were so bright they could run General Motors, and they married. No way were those men their equal. But by golly, they were married. If you were twenty-four and not married yet, you had to leave town."

It was like salmon swimming upstream to spawn. When she did marry, three friends had weddings on the same day she did. When Doris and Truman announced their engagement in 1950, there were a dozen parties. Her mother's friends gave showers. "They went all out over weddings at that time," she said. "It was like a giant trap closing on you.

"I knew I was marrying the wrong person. I remember going to Washington. My father was back in Congress at that point, and I went to get my dress and had my picture taken. Everything had to be done right." She paid $69.95 for the dress. Her father had set a limit of $1,000 for the wedding. An old boyfriend lived in St. Louis. "And on the plane on the way home I would've given anything to have stopped in St. Louis. I wanted to forget the whole thing." But she couldn't.

When Doris and Truman walked out of that church in Omaha in 1951, "We didn't have a word to say to each other. It was a terrible match."

Warren knew Truman well. They were roommates when both were attending the University of Nebraska. And he had helped out on weekends at the gas station young Warren—who had begun building his fortune when he was in knee socks—already owned. "Truman and I were very good friends," Warren said. "He was a very nice guy. He wasn't as bright as Doris, but he was a very decent guy. It would be hard for any man to measure up to my dad. If you were expecting to find my dad and you were my sisters, you would have had a hard time."

Doris had set the bar low as far as her expectations were concerned. "I wasn't expecting anything from Truman. We both were running away from our families by getting married. Off we went with no idea of what it was like to be married or understanding marriage. I just thought you did your duty."

Doris and Truman Wood during Christmas, 1952, on a visit to her parents' home in Omaha. REPRINTED WITH PERMISSION FROM THE OMAHA WORLD-HERALD.

RED BECOMES HER

In 1961, Howard Buffett was slowly dying of cancer, and Doris was distressed that she had so little to talk to him about during her frequent visits. That year, when she was thirty-three, an opportunity arose for her to get involved in political activism, an endeavor that would spark endless hours of conversation with her conservative Republican father. At the same time, it helped her to fully realize that she had both the intelligence and leadership skills to make a difference.

"Nothing really happened to change my inside feelings about myself for years and years and years," she said. "It was only when I got involved in that anti-communism thing that I found out I had any talent at all."

A friend called Doris on a Sunday morning. She had gone to someone's house the night before and watched a documentary about the rise of communism. "She said it was very scary," Doris recalled. Since Doris and her family had lived in Washington, the friend thought she knew something about the threat communism posed. Doris didn't, but her friend still wanted her to help lead a group that would battle the "Red Menace" in Omaha. "I saw the film and talked to my father about it. And he said, 'Do me a favor. Don't say a word until you've studied it for three months.'"

The film did cause her some concern for the future of her children, but the main reason she dove in head first was so her father would be interested in what she was doing, and see her as a political activist in his final days. She read everything she could find on the subject of communism. "It always came back to education," she said. "My father said, 'If the American people are given all the information, they'll always make the right choice.'"

Doris became the group's policy chairman and helped bring in speakers for a five-day seminar. They included Ronald Reagan and Frederick C. Schwarz, an Australian physician who was Executive Director of the Christian Anti-Communism Crusade and founder of a controversial Midwestern anti-communism school. The group's efforts caught the attention of the *Omaha World-Herald*, which did a number of splashy pieces on it, including a feature story on Doris.

She began showing a film, *Communist Encirclement, 1961*, to neighbors and friends.

Doris took out an ad in the *Herald* that struck the same chords that Hillary Clinton's "three A.M. phone call" ad would in the 2008 campaign for the Democratic nomination for president. It began, "Thoughts while tucking your children into bed," and then quoted Lenin. It continued, "For the love of your children, come and hear what Dr. Fred C. Schwarz knows about the Communist Menace."

Doris was pictured on the front page of the paper welcoming Schwarz the morning of the rally, and quoted him as saying the Soviets believed there was no need to attack America, because "the communists are certain it will surrender" without a fight. The morning edition of the

Doris, at right, discovered she had a gift for leadership when she got involved with an anti-communist campaign in Omaha, primarily so she would have something to talk about with her dying father. 1961.

November 17, 1961 *World-Herald* stated that an "amazing" crowd of 7,000 showed up to hear Schwarz. A front-page report said: "With the deft skill of the surgeon he is, Dr. Schwarz exposed the anatomy of communism and made his prognosis: 'The communist conquest is imminent. The impossible will happen. A communist dictator will rule the Earth.'"

The same day's evening edition had a front-page headline that screamed, "Full Support Pledged Anti-Commie School," and showed a smiling Doris with hundreds of telegrams the paper described as an "overwhelming response" in support of bringing the anti-communist school to Omaha.

Her organization had spent just $923 and created a sensation in Omaha. Doris has a scrapbook that includes a dollar bill taped to a 1961 note that reads, "It don't matter who I am. I'm old and I live on a pension, but I hate communism." An editorial in the paper said, "When seven thousand people leave the comfort of home and drive through slush and snow to hear an anti-communist speaker, that means they are very deeply concerned about the communist threat and are looking for information and counsel."

Omaha Mayor James J. Dworak had reservations about the anti-communism school, but bowed to popular sentiment and signed a proclamation of support declaring Omaha "Freedom City, U.S.A.," and made every week of the year 1962 "Anti-Communism Week." Doris had become a celebrity of sorts and caused the mayor to bend to her organization's will, while Warren still labored in relative obscurity.

Later, she would forever be "Warren Buffett's sister." Not so in 1962, when a feature story on her anti-communism efforts in the *World-Herald* mentioned Warren this way: "As the daughter of a Republican congressman and Mrs. Howard Buffett, Doris spent her impressionable teenage years in Washington, D.C., with her parents, a brother, Warren, and a sister, Roberta."

The piece included a smiling picture of Doris and her three children in their Omaha living room. It said she had received anonymous, threatening phone calls, but quoted an undeterred Doris as saying, "The battle against communism is everybody's battle."

Doris with Marshall, Robin and Sydney (in the background) in their living room in 1963 during her anti-communism campaign days. The family had received anonymous telephone threats.

It went on to say she had developed an interest in history while living in Fredericksburg and Washington while her father was in Congress.

By the time the school came to Omaha in May of 1962, she had become a force to be reckoned with in local politics, even though her primary motivation was not a communist threat, but to do something to make her father happy. Doris then became involved in Barry Goldwater's presidential campaign, and was pictured with him in the paper when he came to speak in Omaha.

She went to the 1964 Republican National Convention as an alternate delegate, and had been co-chair of eight states for Goldwater during the primaries. She helped raise money for his general election campaign. She was part

Doris with Senator Barry Goldwater during the 1964 presidential primary campaign.

of a group of young women who had an idea for a "Gold for Goldwater" fundraising campaign, and they were featured on NBC News. "And then I called the doctor and asked how long my father had to live. It wasn't long. So I just stopped campaigning, since the reason I was doing it was to have something wonderful to talk about with him."

When her father passed away at age sixty, her interest in political activism waned. And as the years passed, she and Warren both became somewhere between moderate and liberal politically. But in the process of trying to make her dying father proud of her, she had learned that she could be a formidable leader and could make things happen.

Ironically, those who opposed the anti-communism campaign were sometimes dismissed as "do-gooders." Fifty years later, she had become the personification of the American do-gooder. And when she spoke to students during a 2010 visit to Davidson College to promote her Foundation's "Learning by Giving" campaign—to inspire young people to work for nonprofit organizations across the nation—she made a veiled reference to her days fighting the "communist menace."

"There used to be a myth that communists were trying to take over America by influencing the five percent of college students who were the most intelligent and the most sensitive." She added with a laugh, "Now I'm trying to do the same thing."

Don't Call Her Eleanor

Doris' middle name is Eleanor. But it was never uttered in the staunchly Republican Buffett home after Franklin Delano Roosevelt, a Democrat, was elected president in 1932. The First Lady's name, of course, was also Eleanor. In the height of irony, Doris has made Eleanor's life work of fighting for human rights and supporting working women her own by, among other things, funding education for Afghan girls and providing scholarships, housing and day care for battered women.

Doris' father Howard was a conservative Republican who believed the best government was the least government. He was worried that FDR's New Deal spending that was intended to lift the country out of the Great Depression, could make the dollar worthless. And if that happened, he believed it could result in the nation descending into chaos.

"My father was very good at looking into the future, but he always said his timing was off," Doris said. "He was predicting a war in Korea at a time nobody ever heard of Korea. His basic nature was he didn't like fighting. He didn't think war solved anything. He also thought we ought to mind our own business. There was nothing worth shedding a drop of American boys' blood for."

In opposing President Harry S Truman on the Korean War, Howard said on the House floor: "Even if it were desirable, America is not strong enough to police the world by military force. If that attempt is made, the blessings of liberty will be replaced by coercion and tyranny at home. Our Christian ideals cannot be exported to other lands by dollars and guns."

The Buffett family would have frequent discussions about politics when Howard was in the investment business, and they only became more intense when he was elected to Congress. If Howard, who passed away in 1964, were alive in 2010, he might well have been equally appalled by both George W. Bush and Barack Obama for their spending and military involvement in the Middle East. Today he might be compared to U.S. Representative Ron Paul, a Republican who leans toward libertarianism.

Purely for political reasons, Howard would not have been excited when Doris' genealogical work revealed that the family is related to President Obama—a seventh cousin, three times removed. Doris plans on publishing a book on the Buffett family roots. The book will be wryly titled *A Very Obscure Family*, because a clerk told her it was difficult to find records for the ancestors of the Buffetts, using those very words to make the point. When President Obama and Bertie both happened to be in Hawaii for Christmas 2009, Warren called Doris and he joked, "'Are we having a meeting of kin to which I wasn't invited?' I got a kick out of it," Doris thought it was great. "I was tickled by it."

Many tend to grow more conservative as they get older, not less, especially if they've become wealthy with the passage of time. But Warren and Doris both supported President Obama in 2008 after being raised to be conservative Republicans by a father they adored and respected. Warren has become a major force in the Democratic Party. His public support and fundraising helped give Obama a boost during the 2008 campaign. During the race, Warren told CNBC in May of 2008 that Republican candidate John McCain's support for giving the super-rich tax breaks while the middle class paid a higher rate offended his sense of "social justice."

"As people get older they get more so in most things," Warren said. "If they're nice they get nicer. If they're mean they get meaner. And, in politics, usually as they get older they get more conservative, but not in our case. I'd say that's true of all three of us. We loved our dad so much that anything he said was sort of like coming from God. There was total acceptance."

As they became adults and "we looked at the world around us," their warm feelings about their father didn't change, but their attitudes about his politics did. "We did change political philosophies to some degrees. I think the inequality of the world had an impact upon us. We weren't seeing it through those eyes when we were in high school or when we were in grade school. As we grew older, we saw that the government had an important place not only in fighting wars and delivering the mail, but also in taking care of the people who get the short straws in life."

Bertie said her father's campaigns were exciting for the children. "In the first campaign I was eight years old and I remember going to county fairs. There were five counties that made up the Second Congressional District, and they all had county fairs in the summer. I remember going around with my dad. In those days, campaigns were so simple. We did have one radio spot where we sang 'America the Beautiful' or something. Besides my dad's personal appearances at different places, there were small posters we'd put up on telephone poles. We had these cards that said 'Vote for Howard Buffett' that I'd hand out and say, 'Will you vote for my daddy?' It's so different than now. It was 1942—a long time ago. After handing out a certain amount of them, I would get to ride the Ferris wheel. So that was good."

Doris helping her father, Howard Buffett, campaign for Congress.

Campaign poster shot of the family picnicking. Warren, Howard and Bertie standing. Doris and Leila seated. 1948.

According to his biography, *The Snowball,* Warren accompanied Howard as he campaigned into rough areas where Republicans had never ventured before, including trying to shake hands with tough, staunchly Democratic union workers during shift changes. Warren's job was to run for the police if a fight broke out. He was concerned about the risks that were involved, but he admired his father's courage and integrity.

"It absolutely wasn't a rebellion against the views at home," Warren said of his and his siblings' political change of heart. "It was just opening our eyes, where when we were younger we accepted everything at face value, and then we started forming our own opinions at a given point."

"I didn't change my registration or make any noise until after my dad died," Warren said. "He was sick a long time and none of us would've wanted to do anything to worsen the physical suffering that was taking place. Doris was more active in things in the early '60s that my dad approved of."

"Politics is mainly heart," Doris said. "What you feel." But most of what she was feeling at that time was a desire to make her father happy. Later on, her feelings focused on helping the poor and the powerless.

Warren ran for delegate to the Republican National Convention in 1960, when he was thirty. When his father died, Warren began to move in a different direction. "Civil rights probably had more to do with me shifting than anything else," he said. "It just wasn't something you were conscious of growing up in the early '40s and '50s. There were two different worlds and when they started intersecting— with World War II—the inequities probably hit us all."

Those inequities began to hit Doris when she was ten years old and went to school in Omaha with a boy named Charles Allman, who was from a poor family. "His clothes were clean but tattered. Some people said they ate chicken feed. He was gaunt and didn't look well. I saw the two extremes. I didn't know there were poor people until I met one."

Then there was the cruel treatment meted out to the children of immigrants who ran Dundee's Barber Shop in Omaha, both by their parents and by other kids. "Honest to God, it wasn't human—I can remember their faces because they were trying hard, but there wasn't a chance of them being accepted," Doris said, wiping tears from her eyes.

The only black person the Buffett children knew in Omaha was Ethel Crump, who came to clean their house twice a week. "We adored her. She was a true lady. She had freckles on her nose, was kind and sweet, cheerful and giggled, and a fine person. I had no prejudice."

She encountered racism when she arrived in Fredericksburg in 1943 and was walking down the street with a friend. Van and Louise Holmes, the black couple that "came with" the Payne house the Buffetts were renting—who did the cooking and yard work—were approaching from the other direction. "I said 'Hi,' naturally. And I was told by my white girlfriend, 'Oh, you don't say that' because they were black." Doris was stunned. "I was being told that I shouldn't say 'Hi' in public to people I lived with."

A decade later, Doris was shaken up by something that happened as she was walking down the street in Houston, early in her first marriage: "The sidewalk was wide enough for two people, but the black man walking toward me stepped off the sidewalk onto the street so he wouldn't brush by me or something. It began to dawn on me what it was all about. How terrible to think you have to get off the same sidewalk."

Witnessing things like that shaped the social conscience of the woman who eventually decided to devote her life and her fortune to helping the downtrodden. She became much more politically astute over the years. Doris claims she's an independent, but on social issues and in funding education, she leans Democratic. Education, she said, is our only hope to turn things around.

"When the Constitution was written, there were three million people," she said. "People could pick up a plow or be a blacksmith or a cooper. Those were things you could pick up from your father or work as an apprentice to learn. You didn't need to have a college education. People could support families, find a way to make a living, and the standard of living was lower. I'm concerned that we have more people who are ill-equipped to earn a living and make a life, and I don't know if the government can take care of them. There's waste and inefficiency and corruption and crime in these big programs, and that concerns me."

She said she's no policy wonk and certainly doesn't have all the answers. Doris just thinks about solving problems one person at a time and hopes others will do the same. "I'm not into policy. I'm interested in helping individuals— and outfits that are helping individuals—where I can see that it makes sense. I'm just not smart enough to know about worldwide policies. But I'm concerned about the illiterate and uneducated population that somebody's got to support."

Doris heard a man speak in Denver in the early '50s who said the test of any civilization is how it handles the most vulnerable ten percent of its people. "That always stuck with me. He said the group that's done the best has been the Jewish people. I know that's part of their religion. It's been a tenet of the Christian religion. But it isn't working effectively. My father used to take us to see Indians on the reservation and say, 'That's the perfect example of what socialism is.' So I don't have a policy. I can't think that big. I know what can happen if you bestow a huge amount of money on one particular organization. A lot of things can go wrong. If I understand and believe in the people involved and it makes sense to me, then that's the kind of thing I like to get involved in."

She said her father would have the same reaction to the recent stimulus spending to avert a depression as he did to FDR's New Deal. "I just think he'd be aghast. He was far more concerned about the rise of socialism than he was of communism. He thought we'd lost all our freedoms. He also said once if it got to the point—some percentage—of people who regularly got a check from the government, it was all over. We're way past that now. The world has changed since he died in 1964. I'm afraid he'd be very saddened if he could witness it now."

Black Monday Gives the Black Sheep a Black Eye

Because of her last name, people who have heard about what Doris Buffett is doing invariably assume she was born into a life of wealth and privilege. They think she has no idea what it's like to be poor, or even middle class. They think she's giving away only a small part of her fortune for kicks, while keeping a villa in Italy, a home in the south of France and driving a Rolls-Royce. "It must be nice," they often say.

The truth is she grew up in a solidly middle-class family. When her parents wouldn't let her go away to college, she asked for a car and they said no. After her wedding, she scrimped to get by on her husband's small salary, feeding the family on a food budget of ten dollars a week as they made do with a thirteen-year-old car. Even when Warren was turning her investments with him into millions in the 1970s, '80s and '90s, she continued to clip coupons and do her own washing, ironing and housekeeping.

She still lives a relatively spartan existence for a multi-millionaire, priding herself on finding bargains. She grew up in a frugal family during the Depression. But that's not why she is the way she is. She has nice homes in Fredericksburg and Rockport, Maine. She has indulged in a multi-carat diamond ring. She drives a Volvo. But she doesn't spend as freely as many wealthy people, because the amount she might spend in an afternoon shopping spree could change the lives of a family in need. And for Doris, the latter is much more of a kick than the former.

In 2009, when a man came down to Maryland to talk to her about programs to help troubled youth, he thought it would impress Doris to hear that he'd just invested thirty dollars in a copy of *The Snowball*, Warren's bestselling biography by Alice Schroeder. Doris shot back, "Really? I bought thirty copies at Costco for nineteen dollars each."

The $10,000 Doris had invested in Warren's small fledgling partnership in the early 1950s had been turned into $12 million in Berkshire Hathaway stock by 1987. Yet Warren's genius was both a blessing and a curse. It created wealth. But investors felt you'd have to be a fool to sell the stock, because you knew he'd continue to increase its value faster and faster. There were no dividends, however.

"I was sort of a poor little rich girl," Doris said. She had Berkshire Hathaway stock, and plenty of it. But she was cash poor. "I thought, 'If I sell it now, it's going to go up.' I didn't know about borrowing against it."

Doris became involved with a broker in northern Virginia who was recommended by a friend. "She seemed trustworthy," she said. "She first got me into options. She said that was the way we could create monthly money." Then it became "naked puts," which are very risky. They are promises to cover other people's losses if the market declines. She started out on Black Monday with $12 million in Berkshire Hathaway stock, and by the end of the day she was $2 million in debt. She was sixty years old and divorced.

"I had nothing," Doris said, "just a few pieces of residential real estate, which the clearing house was entitled to. Friends said, 'You have to call Warren,' and I did. I was so ashamed I had done such a dumb thing." She was on the verge of losing her home. But Warren declined to give her money because he didn't want it to go to the people who were soaking her.

"That was a tough situation," Warren said. "I don't know who this woman in Falls Church was, but she not only lost Doris' money but a lot of others'. It wasn't anything people should be doing. I think she got a couple of hundred people to do it. In the end, the money would've gone to the brokerage firm. Doris did have this money that would come when my mother died. But it couldn't be taken before my mother died. It belonged to my mother. In any event, we worked it out so the brokerage firm couldn't seize it and Doris had money to live on."

The Washington Post ran a story on what a poor investor the sister of the Oracle of Omaha was.

A family trust of Berkshire Hathaway stock was to be divided among Doris, Warren and Bertie upon Leila's death. Warren declined to accept his share, so it would be split between his sisters in lump sums over time.

"My brother set up this trust fund to make loans to me, and I had more money than I'd ever had," Doris said. "I couldn't look him in the eye. I never felt so worthless, rejected."

Compounding her investment losses was a real estate fiasco. She had bought a downtown Fredericksburg property from a local attorney with the idea that he was going to remain in what had been the slave quarters adjacent to the main house. The city told Doris they couldn't do that because dividing historic property was not permitted.

The attorney "couldn't or wouldn't" buy her out, she said. "Standoff."

She was so desperate that she asked her mother for help, something that was extremely difficult for her to do. "I said, 'Mom, I need $125,000.' She gave me a check, and the next day she said, 'I want it back.'"

"I was going to have six lawsuits, and I was wiped out. It was just a nightmare." She asked her son Marshall, who was worth millions, and he said no. Initially, Doris felt that everyone in the family "had washed their hands of me."

She began climbing out of her financial hole by moving into the back bedroom of the main house with only a small mattress, a table lamp, and a little stool. "I was in a terrible position."

Then she rented out rooms. At first, "I had a little microcosm of the world—a drug dealer, a girl with multiple sclerosis . . ." But it wasn't all bad. Some of the boarders became lifelong friends. "There wasn't anything I could do for a job at that point. I loved having kids in my house and I ended up with all these college students and recent graduates. We have our own little alumni group."

The wrenching part involved her family. "Warren's first rule is you never lose money, and his second is you never forget the first rule. I probably solidified my position as the family dunce around that time. No disputing that."

When she first met lawyer and husband-to-be Al Bryant, they went to Omaha and she sat outside Warren's office as Bryant talked to her brother. "I couldn't go into his office, it was so painful."

At first, on a visceral level, she couldn't understand why Warren didn't just come riding up like a knight in shining armor and make her worries go away. She would have done that for others in her family if the situation had been reversed. But as time passed, she came to realize it wasn't personal. Warren's businesslike approach to life was the reason she was able to have a good life—and the reason she would later be able to change the lives of thousands of others.

The scare she endured helped "the family dunce" understand the gut-wrenching panic people losing their homes in the economic meltdown of 2008–2010 were feeling as she helped them stay afloat financially. And, how to do that in a way that would teach them to protect themselves in the future—just as Warren had done for her.

THE LITTLE TOW TRUCK
THAT COULD

Brian Fischer, Commissioner of the New York State Department of Correctional Services, was surprised when Doris came to meet with him at the Sing Sing Correctional Facility on the Hudson River in Ossining, New York in 2005, to talk about funding inmate education.

First of all, not many of the people Doris refers to with a smirk as "charitable ladies," are willing to help prisoners. And Sing Sing is not just any prison. It's a maximum-security prison, and a legendary one. The terms "sent up the river," and "the last mile" originated there. But then few, if any, wealthy ladies are like Doris.

"Maybe this sounds terrible, but you always have an image of very wealthy people," Fischer said. "I had no idea of what she would look like or how she would behave. She's such a nice lady. When we see each other every year [at the Sing Sing commencement ceremony], we give a kiss and a hug and ask, 'How's the family?' At the same time, she's the most unpretentious, down-to-earth person that you'd ever want to meet. She's an extraordinary lady. The fact that she gives the money she does to prisons? What can you say?

"Years ago, before I met Doris, I happened to meet another very wealthy person from a well-known family, and she was wearing a necklace with pearls so big you couldn't take your eyes off them. Then Doris comes in with her sweat pants and jacket, and she puts everybody at ease."

Brian told her that every man at Sing Sing had a miserable childhood. They'd received poor educations and little or no parental guidance. He couldn't have known how closely his statements approximated Doris' own watchword of "bad luck through no fault of your own." These men had certainly made bad choices. Some of them had even committed murder. Did they deserve to be helped? They hadn't been prepared as children to make good decisions, particularly to stay off drugs. Still, she had doubts. But when Doris attended Hudson Link-Mercy College's commencement ceremony at Sing Sing, she was so moved she knew this was something she wanted to continue to fund on a big scale, nationwide. She's currently supporting education programs at a dozen prisons.

"She envisions herself as a tow truck," said Jody Lewen, Ph.D., Director of Patten University at San Quentin. "She sees herself as a rescue operation, not in the sense that she's going to pick you up and carry you to safety, but that she's going to get you out of the ditch." Doris gave San Quentin's program a grant in 2006 and again in 2010.

"Other philanthropic organizations judge your cause's sustainability by who your friends and supporters are," Jody said. "Doris judges by who you are."

Doris compared graduating from Sing Sing's higher education program to giving birth. "There's a lot of pain. It takes a long time. But in the end, there's a new life." Sunshine Lady Foundation board member Diane Grimsley attended her first Hudson Link-Mercy College graduation at Sing Sing in 2009. She thought she was prepared for what she would see and hear there. She wasn't.

"I knew it moved Doris beyond words [and] Mitty [Beal, the Foundation's executive director] beyond words," Diane said. "I think it surprised Doris the first time she went. She felt like she watched redemption. Not in a religious sense, but real human redemption. But I was surprised at my gut-level feelings," Diane said. "I was having trouble swallowing. I was having trouble breathing."

An address by the valedictorian, Queens native Todd Matthew Young—who had been convicted of murder in 1988—touched Diane and about 100 others in attendance, deeply. Everyone, including the commissioner, was moved to tears as Young spoke eloquently about a crime committed twenty-three years ago, apologized to his mother, held up his diploma, and told her that for the first time she had reason to be proud of him.

Later, Young told WRNN News Director Richard French, "I never thought I could succeed in this . . . it took many, many years for me to finally get the courage to take the step, because I truly didn't think I could do it. Coming to prison, I thought that was it. It was all over, I was worthless, I didn't have any value. And the word valedictorian means more to me than the regular meaning. It means validation. This is something I should have given my family twenty-three years ago . . . they should have been at this graduation so many years ago. Now it is a blessing of unbelievable magnitude to be able to say, 'Look, I gave you reason to be ashamed. Now here's something to be proud of after all these years.' I'm finally able to show them that they were right in supporting me all this time and not turning their backs on me, as so many other people did."

Fittingly, the 2009 Sing Sing commencement speaker was actor Tim Robbins, who played inmate Andy Dufresne in *The Shawshank Redemption*. Dufresne fought to start a prison library and educate his fellow prisoners in order to free their minds. In the film, Ellis Boyd "Red" Redding, a longtime inmate played by Morgan Freeman, initially admonishes Robbins' character, saying: "Hope is a dangerous thing. Hope can drive a man insane." But he later admiringly describes him as, "Andy Dufresne, who crawled through a river of shit and came out clean on the other side." Robbins called the twenty-eight inmates who received degrees in 2009, "leaders of men" who are bringing hope to their fellow inmates. Excerpts from Young's and Robbins' addresses are included in the next chapter.

Prison college programs always create a political backlash at first. Why should inmates get a free education when people on the outside don't? Even Doris' grandson, Alex, a member of the Sunshine Lady Foundation board, was appalled when he heard she was thinking of funding college educations for inmates. "When she first told me about that program, I didn't like it. Screw these people. Why not pay for an education for someone in a family who'd lost a son or a daughter because of them? But now I've learned there are three million people in prison. And I've seen the program's results. And I've learned the stats about recidivism. I've never been a rubber stamp, saying everything she does is OK. But she's so much of a forward thinker, you realize, 'I need to change how I'm thinking about this.'"

But the money for the programs comes from private grants and donations, not from taxpayers. The college programs actually save taxpayers money. In New York State in 2010, it cost $54,600 annually to incarcerate an inmate, which is about the price of a year's tuition at Harvard University.

As of 2009, forty-nine men had graduated from the Hudson Link program at Sing Sing, and then were paroled. None, so far, had returned to prison. In contrast, the overall New York State recidivism rate was a stratospheric sixty-seven percent, and the national recidivism rate was sixty percent.

"Nationally, all the college programs that exist in prisons have pretty much the same basic data—99.9 percent are very successful in the community," Brian said. "I can understand the community's being uncomfortable with an ex-offender getting a degree," he said. "But the counter argument is that these ex-offenders are coming home. Wouldn't you rather have them coming home educated and fully employed and paying taxes than not educated and run the risk of them returning to crime? I look at this as an investment. It's not a treatment. You get your money back afterward. Society gets it back through public safety and by making them tax-paying citizens."

And college in prison obviously doesn't involve keg parties and sleeping late. "When you go to college in a prison, you don't go to the coffee shop, there's no student unions, there's no late-night rap sessions, you study when you can," Brian said. That's often at four A.M. in their cells when there's finally some peace and quiet.

Brian said they influence other prisoners and even those outside of prison walls in a pay-it-forward fashion. "Once the college programs get started in any institution, other inmates begin to realize that there's more to going to prison than just doing time. And they start to think, 'Maybe I should get a college education'—because the men and women involved in these programs speak so highly about it, and the professors in the programs speak so highly about it, they think, well, maybe that's something I ought to look into. That's one piece.

"The other piece involved inmates talking to their children about education and reading. Some will tell you that it's almost like a competition. The father is going to school and getting a degree and his kids are going to high school, and there's a new give and take and a friendship that in many cases didn't exist before.

"The students in prison encourage and reinforce their children and their brothers and sisters and wives to go back to school or stay in school," Fischer said. "That's a tremendous thing."

Hudson Link for Higher Education in Prison was founded when state and federal funding for college education in prisons ended in the mid-1990s, and inmates at Sing Sing reached out to religious and academic volunteers. Hudson Link restored college education at Sing Sing in 1998 through private funding. Sean Pica, director of Hudson Link, is an alumnus who served sixteen years in prison, the latter part of that time at Sing Sing for murder: "The short version is a girl I grew up with told me at school that her father was doing things [to her] that he shouldn't have been doing. So I put on my cape and flew over and saved the day without thinking about what that meant, and I shot and killed her father." That was in Coram, New York, on Long Island, where Sean grew up.

He entered prison at age sixteen, and received his GED, his associate's degree, his bachelor's degree, and master's degree inside Sing Sing. In order to finish, he had to be part of a group that started up Hudson Link and got the program going again from the inside out, without a cell phone, e-mail or Internet access. "Running a college program is tough," Sean says. "Running a college program within a maximum-security prison is as tough as it gets."

After fourteen months, Pica graduated with a degree in organizational management. He went to work for Hudson Link as the liaison between the current students and the administration. He helped run the office. He did that for about a year, then he went back to graduate school because there was a graduate degree program at Sing Sing as well. While working toward his master's, he continued to work for Hudson Link. In 2002, he went home from Sing Sing. Then he went to Hunter College and earned a master's degree in social work in 2005. In 2007, he was asked to take over as director of Hudson Link.

Sean says studying is difficult at Sing Sing: "The bottom line is that the cell block never sleeps, There's always a certain amount of noise. Even if guys are sleeping, there's toilets, sinks, radios—it's open—it's not rooms. So you have the largest cell block in the world, and on top of that it never stops. So studying in that environment is probably the most difficult kind of situation to study in, ever. The students in the program have no cushy coed study labs, no laptops, no Internet, there's no copy machine. Everything is as difficult as it could possibly be to do the kind of work that they're trying to do." And yet the students do very well.

One Hudson Link alumnus, Za'id Ali, just finished a master's program at Mercy College. He went into Sing Sing as a teenager and got all of his education inside. He came home with a bachelor's degree. Then he went back to Mercy to get his master's in social leadership. It's a one-year, accelerated program on weekends and evenings. He worked full-time throughout. Midway through the three-semester program, Sean checked in with Za'id.

"How's it going?" Sean asked.

"Sean, this is a breeze," Za'id said.

"What do you mean? It's a master's program," said Sean.

"The level of work that I did at Hudson Link at Sing Sing is tougher than what they're asking me to do here for a master's program," Za'id said.

By 2010, Za'id was the Director of the Open Door Medical Center in Ossining. He'd been home about a year. He was doing outreach—HIV/AIDS counseling—in the community, had just finished his master's in social leadership, and he had just become a father.

Doris assisted Za'id with tuition for the master's program. "We have had some unbelievable people who have really taken this on when it wasn't a popular thing to take on," Sean said. "These days, 'reentry' is the buzz word. There are new movies out and reality shows. It's kind of the cool topic to grasp onto now. When it got started, no one wanted to be associated with it. It wasn't popular. It was a tough sell. It didn't make a lot of sense to a lot of people.

"The commissioner, from Day One, said he believed in it and fought to make it happen. Then Ossie Davis, Mayor David Dinkins and Doris Buffett started to come forward. She said, 'I believe in this and I'm going to support it.' None of us really got to know what her motivation was, but we didn't need to."

Jody Lewen said that soon after they met, Doris told her about the plan to give all of her money away by the end of her life. "At the time, I found it bold and refreshing, but now I realize what a loss it will be to the fields she supports, given how few major donors support them at the scale that she does."

One of Jody's colleagues at San Quentin, Jennifer Scaife, happens to be from Fredericksburg. She introduced Jody to Doris, who asked to be sent information on the San Quentin program. "Doris is a relative newcomer to the field of higher education, but is asking all these astute questions," Jody said. "She's picking my brain about what we're doing and how we're doing it for all these other programs. She was figuring out how to be effective making grants that would help prisoners get degrees. She's so smart and so with-it and so far ahead of others. It sounds naïve, but at the time, I thought, 'This woman—it's worth helping her figure out what she wants to do with her money.'"

Then Doris told her she'd decided to give Jody $250,000, on the condition that she incorporate as a nonprofit and have a board of directors that could help her raise money. "Her analysis of who we were and what we needed was so right-on," Jody said. "And she was checking me out personally. 'Is this person competent? Do I feel confident in her abilities?' I think she was also listening for what needed to happen and what was holding us back. Her analysis was that I was buried, spending all of my time fundraising."

When Doris decides a person or project is worthwhile, she usually jumps in and out quickly, preparing the beneficiary to keep going under its own power. "You can have a tremendous impact, even in a short time," Jody said. "She helps very intensively for a short period of time, energizes the organization, and you're deeply inspired and uplifted."

As a result of Doris' involvement, the San Quentin program went through "a phenomenally productive time for us—special events, publications, all these things we've dreamed about. We've got ourselves an office. The question was, 'Are we going to be able to sustain this? Or are we on a prolonged drug trip?' And we're making it.

"There is a risk-taking dimension to what she's doing. You could do what she does and fall on your face. She just believes that people get stuck in ruts, and you just need to shove them hard and they'll fly. And she's combining that theory with an incredible skill set that seems incomprehensible when combined with Mitty's. Mitty's questions are incredibly sharp, incredibly detailed. Most philanthropists are like sheep," Jody added. "She's extremely different, even compared to the Gates Foundation. Very few will give money to support people that almost everybody hates. Doris," she said, "doesn't care what others think and say about her."

Brother Warren has a simple answer for that: "She's got her own scorecard. It's that simple. If she's doing something with somebody at San Quentin, she doesn't care what anybody else thinks about it. She just cares if she gets a good reaction. It's a little bit like how I invest. I do it my own way. And Doris is investing in people. We got that internal scorecard from our father."

Jody said that Doris' boldness in pushing college education in prisons could bring about a sea change. "The question to me is whether she's going to be able to get her brother involved [in prison education]. If she can get Warren to pay attention to criminal justice, even as an economic issue, he could get Bill Gates. It could change the course of U.S. history. It could change the whole landscape." Warren has said he is curious, and plans to attend Sing Sing's commencement in 2010 if he can fit it into his schedule.

Jody said she hopes large philanthropic groups recognize how important the work Doris is doing is: "There seems to be a dynamic there where her stuff is seen as cute, really sweet, and sentimental. You're spending all this time looking at these individuals' lives. But she's also on to something politically that even Bill Gates himself hasn't really locked onto.

"She's being phenomenally effective," Jody said. "She has changed the landscape of prison education nationwide, singlehandedly. She's also very aware of the currency of the name. She didn't grow up with the name having the meaning it has. It's striking to me she is so comfortable, not just using her name, but lending her name. She's giving the person the opportunity to say Doris Buffett gave, and that's really powerful in this field to make it socially acceptable. They don't want to step up and help people who are grossly unpopular. But when they see their peers doing it, it suddenly becomes acceptable. Doris makes political leaders realize that people—even inmates—really matter. Doris knows that if she does this openly, clearly and loudly, it's going to have an impact."

Jody said it's unfortunate that the big philanthropic organizations think it's a bad idea to get directly involved and get their hands dirty. "It's like the difference between aerial bombing and never seeing the individuals, versus hand-to-hand combat on the ground where you see the person's face. On the ground, you're looking people in the eye," Jody said. "The righteousness of those who keep their distance is almost like anti-emotionalism."

THE SING SING REDEMPTION

*A*s already mentioned in the previous chapter, the June 3, 2009 address was delivered by Valedictorian Todd Matthew Young at the Hudson Link-Mercy College commencement exercises at Sing Sing Correctional Facility. Tim Robbins, whose character in *The Shawshank Redemption* started a prison education program, also spoke to the gathering.

Here is an excerpt from Young's address:

> President Teddy Roosevelt was quoted as saying, "A man with no education can steal a freight car, but a man with a college education could steal the entire railroad." [Audience laughs.] Maybe that quote was not the best one for this situation. . . .
>
> Twenty-three years ago, when I should have been graduating from college, making my family proud, seeking my niche in the world, where I might make my dent in life, I was instead walking around with a chip on my shoulder. Thinking no one could teach me anything. I was very much a punk and a cocaine addict. In my selfish state of arrogant ignorance, raging against my wounds, real and imagined, I took the life of another human being. For this despicable act, I was deservedly sent to prison.

Prison is very much a survival game, and I arrived equipped with attitude and some street smarts, enough to survive the worst of it. I thought to make the best of my lifelong confinement and loss of freedom I faced. I knew I had no future, simply an existence. I was a used-up Coke bottle, if you will, my niche on the trash heap, making my dent in the landfill of life.

In today's world, environmental concerns are at the forefront. We are all "going green" by respecting the planet, avoiding waste of resources, developing alternative energy sources and recycling. Well, we here in Sing Sing have gone green for years now!

Unfortunately, we live in a world where instant gratification is the norm and if something does not perform to expectations, it is replaced, rather than repaired—a disposable world. The majority of society views prison as a landfill hill of disposable people, good for nothing. I thought society had sent me to the dump where unwanted trash belongs—that's how I felt—fully deserving to rot away, not fit for civilization. The weight of all my bad choices, errors in judgment, addiction, disgrace to my family, angry violent behavior, had me fully convinced I was where I belonged. What other company could I expect than to hang out than with other disposables on the garbage pile? It is not difficult to endure prison when you know what you did and hate yourself as a result. You feel you have no value; you make your niche in the landfill.

However, God had another plan, and He always "goes green." My wife Lauren showed me the road to begin forgiving myself because she saw something in me, some potential, and some possibility. Lauren encouraged me to try college. And Mercy met me there. All of you who support education in prison look at the landfill as a recycling center. You see

*potential and strive to provide us with the refining process nec-
essary to nurture it. It isn't easy and it is not always pretty.*

*The recycling process can be downright painful. First,
scrubbing away the memories of past failures. Then removing
the labels of criminal, convict, loser, trash and felon. Sani-
tizing away the bacteria of ignorance, insecurity, doubts
and self-deprecation. Smashing the stigmas of poverty, the
drop-out mentality, addiction and violence. Heating things
up, raising the bar, skimming off false belief systems and
damaging negativity; purifying and empowering with knowledge and truth—melting fears and replacing them with hope
until we are transformed into new, useful and valuable
resources—fit for society and able to shine. Education is our
recycling center.*

*When I first started college I truly didn't think I could do
it: I didn't believe I could succeed, I wasn't a good student,
couldn't do math, would never amount to anything—but
Mercy [College] met me there. So what has college done for
me? What have my professors helped me to realize through
their teaching efforts? I have a broader perspective in my
outlook. I have an increased ability to communicate effectively in many mediums, greater compassion for people, pride
in the accomplishments of others, increased self-esteem, confidence, discipline and a greater sense of myself as a person:
I now feel that I am just as good as anyone else, yet better
than none. I have a vision for a future full of prospects, the
ability to think critically—see the bigger picture—a deep-
ened ability to love myself, others, my wife and family. A
passion to improve, to achieve, a desire to help others reach
their goals and an overarching desire to give back to society,
to become a positive, galvanizing influence on the world.*

*The examples shown to me by my professors have
enabled me to realize I have a gift to teach, to help others*

gain an understanding of sometimes difficult material. I charge my fellow graduates today to take the gift that has been bestowed and help someone else. Reach back into the landfill and give a hand up to another person.

Knowledge should not be allowed to stagnate. Instead, it needs to be shared, like the love of God: The only way you can keep it is to give it away. The more you help others, the more you learn. Trust me, you can do it. You should do it. You must do it. If only to prove to yourself that you have changed. Transformation affects much more than just ourselves.

Education has had such a profound effect on me one might think I would forget that Coke bottle I used to be but I don't ever want to forget. George Santayana said that "those who forget history are doomed to repeat it." I never want to repeat my history. We as prisoners have long thought that having a record was a strike against us, but I suggest that it can be a blessing as well. We will be reminded of where we have been and our past will be foremost in our minds.

So, gentlemen, don't forget where you have been! Don't forget the sacrifices made on your behalf to get you here. Don't forget the heartaches and sorrows you caused your family, your victims and their families. Don't forget the debt you owe to those who have gone before and those who come after you. Antoine Doran, Lloyd Naraine and Bhisham Persaud, you are the youngest graduates here today. You are doing the right thing and that is commendable, but don't forget you are role models and you represent more than just yourselves. Don't forget the words of Abraham Lincoln who said, "Bear in mind, your own resolution to succeed is more important than any other thing."

It is not what is done to you that determines your outcome, but what you do next. You can decide to let the past go and accept responsibilities for your actions and reactions. When you do this you take back your power, open yourself to new options and make choices that position you to come out of it stronger, wiser and more blessed. Mr. Rogers, the famous TV show host, said, "We know deep down that what matters in this life is more than winning for ourselves. What really matters is helping others win, too!" Barack Obama agreed with this idea when he said, "Our individual salvation depends upon our collective salvation." To put it simply, we need each other . . .

As much as it is important that I remember I have "gone green," I wish I could somehow erase from the life of my mother the memories of the pain and shame I caused her. Mom, I have given you numerous reasons to be ashamed of me. Today I give you reason to be proud. You see, you did do a good job with me: It just took a while to show. I vow that this is the first of many more [proud moments], and I vow to be a son you can be proud of. I love you. . . .

To conclude, Warren Buffett once said, "Chains of habit are too light to feel, until they become too heavy to break." That is a profound observation. For years, I felt those chains, but now my former chains have been cast off, replaced with a new chain, one forged of Hudson Links: links of confidence, compassion, selflessness, generosity and empathy, a chain linking me to success. One day soon I will exit these gates to find my niche out there—like Sean Pica, Gregory Frederick, Mark Wallace, Marvin Ramos, Za'id Ali and others. And like them, I will bring honor to my mother, my sister, my friends and family. And maybe, restore honor to that life that was lost at my hands 23 years ago. Oh, and that Coke bottle that I once was? It has been recycled into pure, crystal-clear valedictorian glass. For that I thank you all, and God Bless.

Inmate Todd Matthew Young's 2009 valedictorian address delivered at the Hudson Link-Mercy College commencement ceremony at Sing Sing moved everyone in the room to tears, including New York State Commissioner of Corrections Brian Fischer. HUDSON LINK.

Actor Tim Robbins of The Shawshank Redemption *with inmate graduates after he spoke at the 2009 Sing Sing commencement ceremony.* HUDSON LINK.

Robbins had the twenty-eight inmate graduates roaring with laughter when he talked about a possible sequel to *The Shawshank Redemption*, and he praised the concept of rehabilitation through education that Doris is supporting.

Here is an excerpt from Robbins' address:

I broke out of Shawshank Prison in a dramatic fashion that wound up with the warden committing suicide for his transgressions and me living out the sweet life with a bad ass boat and my best friend Red, in Zihuatanejo, Mexico. People have often fantasized what the sequel to Shawshank Redemption *would be and the best I can come up with is entitled* Red and Andy: Girls Gone Wild, Zihuatanejo. *But that would just be a cheap way to make loads of cash that would betray the moral center of a beautiful story.*

At the heart of Shawshank *is the idea of hope. That despite the cards you have been dealt, whether you are innocent or guilty, whether you wound up in this prison by just or unjust means, that everyone is equal within these walls and that everyone possesses the same potential of spirit. That all within these walls have lives to live, choices to make, love to give and love to receive. That beyond the transgressions and oppression of the incarcerated life there is always the possibility of liberation, of freedom. And that freedom doesn't come from prison breaks or drugs, or idle fantasy, but from the transformative power of the mind, the transformative power of the written word. No one knows that more than you.*

I'm in the business of entertainment. I have seen many movies and read a lot of scripts that put forth the idea that what makes a character develop into a new layer of cool is a sexy car chase, a kick-ass fight scene, and scoring the hot chick. And believe me I know and accept the responsibility of how that errant moral representation of reality may have affected your lives. But I think it is relevant to this ceremony tonight and indicative of the necessity of Mercy College to point out that the most popular movie of our time has as its arbiter of cool the opening of a library built by inmates at Shawshank prison.

There is a beautiful heart in the United States. It strains against the noise of the reactionary voices that cheapen it. This beautiful heart is told to punish and to lock up those that threaten our way of life. This beautiful heart is not asked to look at the individual or the possibility of transformative change. This heart is told to hold resentment and to forget and give up on those who have fallen. But whenever this heart knows, whenever this heart sees, whenever this heart feels the specific, the individual, the human being holding on to hope, the possibility of redemption, this heart rises, this heart celebrates, this heart believes. I know this in my own heart. I know it from seeing the tremendous dedication of Bruce Macleod and Hudson Link to the idea of transformative change. I know it from the tireless and altruistic spirit of Dr. Kimberly Cline and the professors and educators who give their time and their lives to this program. I know it from witnessing the forward-thinking philosophy of Commissioner Brian Fischer and Superintendent Dawson Brown and I know it from looking at you, the Mercy College graduates of 2009.

I also know that this beautiful heart exists in America at large because of my experience in the years after Shawshank Redemption's release. I can't tell you how many people have approached me in the past 14 years with a deep and profound appreciation of how Shawshank has affected their lives, changed their lives. They sometimes get the name wrong; I've heard how deeply moved they are by

Scrimshaw Reduction, *how they just saw* Shankshaw *for the 20th time, how their favorite movie of all time is* The Shrimpshack's Retraction. *But their sentiment is clear. There is something profoundly important about this movie to many people's lives. I have been humbled by the response to the film and honored to hear people's reactions. At first I couldn't quite figure out what it was about the film that had touched this collective heart. Was it that this film told the story of a real friendship, a love between two men that didn't rely on fast cars or skirt-chasing? Was it about the idea that hope could overcome the oppressions of life and set people free? Or was it that the film gave life to all those lessons in our various religions about forgiveness and compassion and transcendent redemption and provided the possibility to us that these elusive concepts can be truly felt and practiced in our everyday lives? I don't know. I would like to believe that our better selves are desperate for stories that embrace the true nature of forgiveness and understand that Christ at Calvary spoke his last words of compassion on Earth to two convicted felons. I do believe that there are countless hearts throughout the world that are open to love and forgiveness and that when fairness and justice may fail us that we can always count on the miracle of the human heart to deliver us.*

I had the good fortune and privilege in 1995 to meet a woman, a Catholic nun who made me not only forgive all the Catholic nuns who had rapped my knuckles and made my life miserable in grade school, but also opened my eyes to the deeper mission of what it is to be a person who has dedicated her life to the life and lessons of Jesus. Sister Helen Prejean had written a book called Dead Man Walking *that told of her experience with death row inmates in Louisiana. In the book she talks honestly about the dilemma she* encountered as she took on the role of spiritual advisor to prisoners about to die at the hands of the state.

She talks about the outrage she faced from the families of the victims of the men she was counseling and the guilt she felt from this. She talks about her struggle to come to terms with the crime that the inmates she was advising had committed. There is a passage in the book that took hold of me, that made me understand why this story needed to be told and it was this: "Every man is worth more than his worst day." Every guilty man in a prison today is in there for his weakest moment, his gravest mistake, his lesser self, a moment, a failing, a misguided path he chose to follow. In writing this, Sister Helen wasn't making excuses for the sin or trying to advocate for an inmate's release. She was simply reminding us that there are human failings, however brief, that result in lasting consequences, and that these moments of failings should not be the true and entire representation of the man. That despite his crime there is, underneath society's hatred of his transgressions, a possibility for that man to rise above his past and become whole again. That every man is capable of rising up to his better self and defining himself not by his moment of weakness but by his dedication to his strength and his commitment to change. This is something that I don't need to tell you, you that are graduating today. You know this in every cell of your body. You know this in your soul.

You have risen beyond the shackles of limitations and judgment. You have looked fear and intimidation and self-doubt in the eye and forced it to its knees as you have taken your books in hand to educate yourself and rise above what was expected of you. I am humbled and honored to be in your presence today on this momentous and auspicious occasion that celebrates your tremendous achievement. You are an inspiration to us all. This isn't a graduation ceremony of kids that have been entitled with their achievement by the ordinary and obligatory idea that higher education is a birthright of the wealthy. This is an achievement that carries with it the true commitment you have showed, regardless of the obstacles and challenges placed before you. This is a college education that is truly earned without the frills of frat rushes, homecoming football games or keg parties, an education that is wholly an education and not an idle four-year distraction, an education and an enlightenment that will inform your future years with a beautiful light, a beacon that will illuminate a redemptive road.

That piece of paper you will hold in your hand is pure light, an acknowledgement of how truly unique and special you are. That piece of paper represents your unbridled power, your limitless potential. You have the power now to change lives by your example, to protect those who might fall and to lift those up who have fallen. You have the power to inspire others, to guide others, to teach, to nurture, to love with compassion. That piece of paper holds a lot of potential in it. Believe in it, live it, celebrate its importance and celebrate your significance. You have become the catcher in the rye, a leader of men, a guardian angel, a protector, a provider and a shining light of this beautiful brotherhood that has flourished within these walls. May your future hold no boundaries to your spirit.

For some reason, Warren was able to let his mother's criticism roll off his back. But it wrapped its tentacles around Doris, squeezed hard and never let go. "In the end," Warren said, "If my mother told me I was no good, I thought, 'What does she know?' I preferred my father's opinion. That might've been much tougher for Doris." Settling for Truman Wood, a man she didn't love and didn't really want to marry, seems to be evidence that it was.

Both of Truman's parents had drinking problems. His father, Ben Wood Jr., passed away in 1932, when Truman was young. His grandfather, Truman Ellsworth Stevens, a prominent businessman in Omaha, sent Truman's mother, Dorothy Stevens Wood, who had been a flapper in the 1920s, away to Denver, along with her son Truman. He provided a $50,000-a-year allowance, but he was embarrassed by her high-profile cavorting. When Truman's grandmother, Belle Weeks Stevens, died, his mother returned to Omaha "to take care of Gramps."

"We were both escaping our mothers," Doris said. "We both knew we had to get married. My family looked so secure—his family was a mess—and I suspect that was very attractive to him. I was led to believe I was dumb. And

Truman was a very nice person, but—not to be mean about this—he flunked out of law school. I didn't think I was fit material for somebody who graduated from Harvard. I had lots of boyfriends because I was really good looking—but I didn't realize that, either."

Now another ingredient was added to the mix. Truman and Doris had gotten away from home, but that didn't make them feel better about themselves or provide direction to their lives, beyond doing what you were supposed to do in the 1950s—set up housekeeping and have babies. Their circumstances had changed, but they hadn't.

"No question about it," Doris said. "Truman didn't have a mean bone in his body, but he was depressed. I was probably depressed. He had very low expectations for himself now that I look back. His mother told him that he would never have to work because of his grandfather's money. And finally he decided he didn't have to work."

It was a time long before the constant bombardment of TV ads for antidepressants.

"I didn't really know the word 'depressed,'" Doris said. "You did what you were supposed to do. It didn't really matter if you were depressed. I wasn't the moody one in the family. That was my sister. I was Mary Sunshine. That was my role in the family. We all have roles in families. I'm sure I was depressed, but I didn't know it," she said. "There wasn't any fun in my life—I knew that. I married someone without a sense of humor, and that was a bad thing to do in my case. None of my husbands had a sense of humor." Doris, who had always been so good at making others laugh, was living without laughter in her life.

More than two decades passed before Doris saw a psychologist. He diagnosed her with mild depression. "When I was finishing up with him, he said, 'When you walked into this office you had one view of yourself and I had mine, and it was radically different than yours. And I had to pull them together.' Yet to some degree, I was still feeling inferior at fifty."

But in the 1950s and early 1960s, Doris kept a stiff upper lip and soldiered on. They moved to Denver, and Truman took a job with Continental Oil, then transferred to Houston. Money was tight. In the beginning, Truman made $260 a month. The most he earned was $630 a month.

"I was eager to have children because that was the next step," Doris said. She said she would have been happy to have gotten pregnant on their honeymoon. They had three children, Robin, Marshall and Sydney. Truman's depression continued to worsen until he no longer got out of bed. Since he had been told he would never have to work, he eventually sank to a point where he decided he either no longer would, or could. He quit when he was thirty-four and never worked another day.

Around that time, Doris began to gain confidence through her work as a leader of the anti-communism group in Omaha. One day, when Truman asked Marshall, "What's *wrong* with you?" in a hurtful way, she reached escape velocity. "That's a terrible thing to say to a child. I thought, 'I can't live like this anymore.' I didn't know what we were going to live on." The only way out was the money she made on her initial $10,000 investment early on in Warren's partnership.

Soon after Doris divorced Truman—after fifteen years of marriage—the inheritance he had been promised came through. But it wouldn't have mattered if it had materialized earlier. Doris knew it was time to leave him, even though divorce was socially unacceptable at the time. The night she told the children, she was putting ten-year-old Marshall to bed, and he said, "Momma, if you find a nice man and want to marry him, it's OK with me."

"I thought that was so sweet. I wish it would have worked out that way. It was really hard on them." She didn't want to uproot the children. So she stayed in Omaha for a while after the 1966 divorce.

"We had a wonderful neighborhood of young parents and children the same age. But all our neighbors were peeling off and moving to bigger houses, because these were small homes, and that certainly wasn't going to happen to us. One couple would put on a musical every summer with the kids in the neighborhood, like *Sound of Music*. We had just superb neighbors. It was a golden age for the children." But there were few single men in Omaha at the time.

"Somebody fixed me up with a date and he was a football coach in a high school, but we just didn't have anything in common. It was a small town I grew up in and I thought, 'This just isn't working.' I thought back to Washington. I thought back to all the wonderful things I really loved—the Smithsonian, history, architecture and all of that."

So she packed up the kids in 1967 in her Pontiac convertible and left for D.C., where she was a neighborhood novelty—the only divorced woman. "So the neighbors had to check me out. I made some good friends that year. I was so encouraged." There she met George Lear, in 1968, on the steps of the Fourth Presbyterian Church, which she thought might be an omen. He was divorced, with four daughters. And he was everything Truman wasn't.

"In the first place, he was a hell of a lot smarter than Truman, which was encouraging," Doris said. He was a lieutenant colonel in the Army—a West Point graduate, and an atomic engineer in the Corps of Engineers. Her father had told her she needed to find a father for the children. "So I was following his orders, once again"; and, doing her duty, they married.

Things went fine for a while. Then, one weekend when Doris was away with Sydney on a trip, George tried to sleep with Robin—who was eighteen at the time. That, said Doris "was the end. There's no going back when that happens." Her divorce from George became final in 1975. "When people ask now why I don't dismiss people who are in prison, I tell them there was a time in my life when, if I had a gun, I would have shot someone." That someone was George.

In 1978, she married a University of Colorado professor named Edward Rozek. Edward, a native of Poland, was a well-known intellectual and anti-communist. "I was alone," Doris said. "The kids had all gone their own ways and I was very lonely. I didn't love him, but he was very intense and very interesting. And he was a fast talker."

It wasn't long before he tried to keep Doris under his thumb. When they went to parties, Edward would sternly tell her with whom she could talk and for how long. And he would accuse her of being interested in other men. The end came when Edward hosted a lavish party for his faculty colleagues and wealthy Denverites. When it was over, he told Doris to write him a check for $12,000, to cover the cost of the party. Then she discovered that the university had already paid the bill. That caused her to begin questioning everything he did. Then, Doris found some documents from his office that seemed to show a pattern of using questionable methods to raise funds.

They divorced in 1980, and she cooperated with the Boulder district attorney's office. In 1983, Edward was charged with twenty-two felony counts, including theft, embezzlement, forgery and charitable fraud. When his attorney accused the special prosecutor of outrageous conduct in the investigation, he stepped aside. Edward was given a deferred prosecution—amnesty for fulfilling certain requirements.

And Doris was advised that he was about to file a lawsuit, and that she and the special prosecutor in the case could expect to be served. "I was the one with the deep pockets," she said. "I felt he had controlled enough of my life and I didn't want to get mired down in that, spending a lot of time in court." She was in Washington at the time and decided to leave town to avoid being served. She was told that Edward's attorneys would be on the lookout for her at the airport. Doris was having dinner at a friend's house, and the friend had an idea to help her slip out of town undetected. She knew where she could get a nun's habit. "And those are hard to come by," Doris said. "You can't just go into a store and buy one." The habit was taken in so it was a perfect fit. Doris even went to a Goodwill store to find the kind of purse that nuns carried. "The woman working in the store looked at me and I knew she must've been thinking I had decided to go into a convent, but she didn't want to ask."

The disguise worked. Doris made it onto the plane undetected. "I was the Flying Nun," she said with a laugh. "It was a lot of fun."

She met Alfred Scales Bryant, an attorney who lived in Morehead City, North Carolina, when she was trying to sort out the mess her finances had become after the 1987 stock market crash. They hit it off and married in 1989. "He had kind brown eyes," she said. "He was just very polite and courtly." And it was a time when she needed some kindness and concern, because she believed her family was ashamed of her. They moved to Morehead City, a beach town so small that even the McDonald's restaurant closed when summer ended.

"I envied them," said Diane Grimsley, a longtime friend of Doris' from her days in Morehead City (later to become a board member of SLF). "I remember sitting here and watching the way he looked at her. He absolutely adored her. When they first moved here it looked like they were deeply in love. It was really sweet. Maybe four or five years into the marriage, things began to change."

When Doris became ill in 1999 and went into the hospital, her friend Peggy Britt of Chapel Hill noticed something odd. "Al didn't seem to comfort her physically. There was no kind of physical contact. He didn't hold her hand." When they entered the hospital, Al walked ten feet in front of Doris.

When Doris was diagnosed with colon cancer, she learned that Al was seeing a number of other women. She found love letters on the fax machine in their home. "I didn't see that coming," she said. "And looking back, I didn't see how I could have failed to see it. There were so many signs, so many clues. But he was good at talking his way out of things. He was a trial lawyer."

Bryant was out of town when Doris discovered the evidence of his infidelities. Her grandson Alex was with her at the time. "I was there when she found out about all that and she was so businesslike," Alex said. "She controlled her emotions. She got her attorney, got her friends mobilized. She got everything together and got the whole thing done, and served him when he got off the plane."

Doris collected all of Al's belongings and put them in a storage facility. "It was like she was not just going to lie there and turn up her toes and weep," Peggy said. "She gathered her friends around her. She didn't let herself be victimized. She got a private investigator on it."

Doris went to the local Walmart where one of the women Al was seeing worked. At the end of their talk, the two women gave each other a hug. "She was an older woman with no money who lived in a trailer, and I felt sorry for her," Doris said.

Bryant, the only one of Doris' husbands who was still living at this writing, declined to be interviewed for this book.

"I never understood why she was with Al," Alex said. "He was never good enough for her." He'd call her "Babe," which gave Alex the creeps. "He just had this way of talking to her and about her as if it were a different time, like she was the doting housewife, like she was not the smart one. I didn't see her that way. She was this powerful, strong, hyper-intelligent, motivated woman who did all these things."

She divorced Bryant in 1999, ten years to the day after they married. "I like the symmetry of that," her divorce lawyer joked. Coincidentally, her marriage with Rozek had lasted exactly two years. "I had two marriages that were door to door, ending on anniversaries," Doris noted wryly. "I should be in the *Guinness Book of World Records*.

"I've done very well choosing friends and very poorly with husbands," Doris said. "But I had a different gauge for judging them. That's the way I've got it figured out." She said she tells herself, "Stick to the friends, Doris, and every-thing will be fine. . . ."

My Prediction? Pain!

Doris blamed her poor choices in men for the strained relations with her children that developed when they were teenagers, and grew worse as they became adults. "It was really hard on them," she said, when she divorced Truman. She tried to stay in Omaha to make things easier, but finally, she had to leave.

"I've rethought that and rethought it and rethought it," she said. "As awful as it was, I don't know what would've happened if I'd stayed in Omaha." At every family gathering, she was the only single person. It was so pitiful that Leila tried to help by inviting Doris to join her much older bridge group.

"I had only one friend who was single—or divorced, I should say—and her life was worse than mine. It was a pretty miserable situation. I figured if I could do things of interest to me, that would be better for the kids. Maybe that was selfish—I don't know. Those nights playing solitaire 'til three A.M. were really grim."

While Warren wasn't that involved with Doris' children, he observed: "When you've got tough marriages, it can't be good for the whole family unit. I've seen that elsewhere. Kids are going to know and react to difficulties that the parents have. I see Marshall. Not that often, but he reminds me of his dad in some ways. He's a very sweet guy. Sydney, I don't see her. I don't know what's going on with Robin. It can't be easy for children when marriages break up."

"Marshall's very socially aware," Doris said. "Always has been. He was able to get the nuances as a little kid. Mothers will tell you babies have characteristics when they come out of the womb, and they endure. Marshall makes speeches. He's always been verbal and very proud of that. He can come up with some great lines. He always used to have a good sense of humor." She last saw him in 2008 at a Berkshire Hathaway annual meeting. He has done well with his shares, she said.

"Sydney," Doris said, "was my sweetheart. I saw her in 2004 when Susie, Warren's first wife, died. She came to the funeral. It was very brief. I don't think there were any words exchanged. She brought her second child—a little boy—and he was as cute as can be." Sydney Wood, who lives in Greenville, South Carolina, didn't respond to efforts to interview her for this book.

The Executive Director of the Sunshine Lady Foundation, Mitty Beal—who is also one of Doris' friends—said of the situation: "I don't know, I find it to be so painful to even contemplate that I block it out of my mind. I think that she just has blocked it out. She has decided to protect herself around her kids and in her mind tries not to go there. I just can't imagine it. She has become so afraid of being hurt again and again and again, that at her age she's decided that she's not willing to risk it. It's not something that I can identify with or can grasp, but I imagine that the pain is immense. And not just for her, but for the kids, too."

Doris had left for Washington after her divorce from Truman. Truman's inheritance provided for $150 a month in child support. "He had moved to Florida. Later it was changed to $300 a month, and then I never got any. He didn't pay. He didn't have to. His trust was set up in Nebraska and he lived in Florida. He never went back. I checked into it. There was no way."

Truman seemed to want to punish Doris for the divorce, and mental illness apparently remained a factor. "He caused me a lot of worry about the children." He came to Washington and stayed at a motel, visiting the children and holding Sydney's head underwater in the pool and scaring her, Doris said. When the children visited him in Florida, she said that Marshall, then a young boy, called her from a phone booth crying hysterically, saying, "Daddy this and Daddy that"; and the final line was that he saw his headlights coming, and he hung up.

"So what are you going to do? They would describe how sometimes at night he would drive them around in the car with a bottle of liquor between his legs and turn the headlights out. I was just terrified for their safety. It was really hard."

Truman also played a game in which he would tell the children he had sent them a letter and that Doris must have thrown it out. "The first letter was labeled '1' and the second letter was labeled '4.' He was playing mind games."

"All right, it was dirty pool," Robin Wood said about her father's actions toward her mother. "He had a lot of problems." Robin said she had butted heads with Doris since she was a teen, because she believed her mother had blown Robin's problems out of proportion; while Doris has felt that Robin was too hardheaded to listen.

"Sydney," Robin said, "is difficult. Sydney has always been difficult." So Sydney and Doris clashed well before the teenaged years.

Marshall and Doris began fighting, Robin said, because "he'd smoke pot in junior high. He was a musician. She was worried about him. She didn't understand what marijuana was." A frightened Doris was from a time when no one did things like that.

A pivotal moment for Robin arrived when she was eighteen, the night when George, who had been drinking, tried to get in bed with her while Doris and Sydney were out of town. Doris said she has never cried as much as she did when she heard about the incident. Though she divorced George, she couldn't erase that moment. Robin said at first she didn't think the incident would have a lasting impact, but that it has bothered her for years. "Up until she was eighteen or nineteen, she was an impressive individual," her brother, Marshall Wood, of Norwell, Massachusetts, said. "Robin was bright and adept. One day, Mom walked into the room and said, 'You've got to drive to Vassar and go pick up Robin. She's dropping out of college.' I was eighteen or so and looked at it as a road trip. I had no knowledge that my sister was dropping out of college because she was depressed. In many ways, she wasn't the same person after that. I always felt very sad about that. Up until then she was a powerhouse."

Marshall became Tony Bennett's bass player. "I've been sober and clean—I haven't had a drink or a drug—since 1985," he said in 2010. "Music was an intelligent choice for me and I've risen to the top of my field."

He said he was never addicted to any drug, but that it might be fair to say that he had a drug problem: "Oh, there might have been, then. In 1974, a lot of American youth were experimenting with drugs because *Time* magazine and other publications were reporting—and the general consensus was—that marijuana wasn't that bad for people. Well, it turns out that marijuana is horrible for people. I had read that cocaine seemed to have no discernible health risks and it turned out to be an incredibly destructive drug. So I wasn't any different than anybody in our neighborhood. I was a late bloomer in that respect.

"The standard in our family has always been my grandfather, and it's a standard I admire and adhere to as well. My grandfather was this amazing and moral person. So somebody smoking pot who is the grandson of Howard Buffett was just very difficult for my mother to comprehend or to accept. Fair enough—that makes sense. But it got blown out of proportion, and then it became sort of my identity as far as she was concerned, and it really wasn't. So it probably made it pretty tough for her to see the forest for the trees. She just saw me as somebody who smoked some pot."

Doris' divorce from his father created a huge upheaval in the children's lives, Marshall said. "We went from Omaha, Nebraska, to Washington, D.C., and I was like a country bumpkin. I'd never been around people moving that fast. I immediately got into difficulties as a small child, as a ten-year-old in Washington. That sort of set the tone. There was a succession of husbands and those marriages always ended with great drama, as did her first. The drama always involved the three kids. That drama had a lasting impact on all of us.

"My father was an inept father because he had no father. And he lived with a mother who had a mental illness and a brother who probably also had a mental illness . . . My dad was pretty frantic around the time my parents got divorced and he probably wasn't properly medicated, so he was fairly manic at that point. Most of his life was spent in depression, but there was a lot of mania up until he was treated and stayed on his medication around 1968 or 1969."

Marshall said he believed depression has played a role in their family's problems from the beginning. Robin talks openly about her longtime battle with it. Doris said she has been treated for it. And Marshall said he suspects that Sydney suffers from "depression with some mania." Marshall said he believes his relationship with drugs involved an effort to self-medicate his depression. He said he had developed a regimen that was holding the disease at bay, and he felt good. "There seems to be an incredibly high incidence of depression in our family. We have a lot of people in the Buffett family that have had great bouts of depression."

Through the years, Marshall said, he lost the connection to his mother.

Robin married Christopher Rozek, Edward's son, and put him through law school by selling shares of Berkshire Hathaway. They had a son, Alexander Buffett Rozek. Robin and Christopher divorced, and she moved to Fredericksburg. Christopher had convinced their eight-year-old son Alex that his mother and grandmother were "evil," and Alex chose not to see them from the time he was in the fifth grade to the tenth grade, while he lived just forty-five miles away in Washington with his father.

Robin married Mark Haymes in Fredericksburg. During the time Alex was out of her life, her struggle with depression worsened. That continues to worry Alex, whose grandfather Truman killed himself after suffering from depression, and then Parkinson's disease. Robin and Mark later divorced.

By 2010, Doris was taking care of Robin financially—but with the condition that she continue treatment for what Robin herself says is clinical depression, keep house and get a job. Robin had been caring for two elderly people part-time. She said that after suffering from depression for years, she had begun to feel better and was ready to get what she called a "real" job.

"My grandmother loves her daughter," Alex said. "Mom loves her mom. There's no question about that." Robin said she loves Doris, but added, "Love is not conditional." Alex replied that, "There are strings attached in life. Life is conditional." He feels his mother could have lost five to ten years that she might have had with Doris because she wasn't properly diagnosed and treated. His mother and grandmother share common interests in history, architecture, art and antiquing, and could have spent many happy hours together over the years. And he's sad that Robin has skipped Berkshire Hathaway annual meetings for years. "All the times we've been out to Omaha, people would ask, 'How's your mother?' She could have been there. They would have loved to see her. It's just such a shame, such a waste.

"For the last nine years, my grandmother and I have gone through I don't even know how many plans to try to help my mom. We've sat down with a trust attorney and tried to set up a trust—with incentives. That sounds bad. Whatever you make, we'll double it or triple it. Work at an art museum. Volunteer on an archeological dig. Just do something to try to get it going. My grandmother's never quit. She's never said, 'That's it. I'm done.'"

It could also be said that Robin never quit on Alex. By the time he was entering his teens, it became obvious to him that his father wasn't telling him the truth. When he returned to her, he found that Robin was a loving, nurturing mother.

"Christopher was vindictive," Robin said. "He knew if he kept Alexander away from me that would hurt me.

It was really hard for those five years. Alexander's coming back was a huge event in my life." When his father had custody, his mother was supposed to see him three weekends a month and in the summer. "That never happened," she said. Yet Robin kept reaching out to Alex.

"Anyway, I didn't see him," she said. "That was agony. I have to say that I got to the point where I didn't even say I had children. Because how do you explain that? So when I got the call from Christopher to take him back, I think I was up there, oh, in about three hours, and Alexander came back from Maryland to live with me. I always had a room for him. I was always ready for him."

Ultimately, Marshall said of Doris, Sydney, Robin and himself, "I don't think that anyone in our story seeks to do evil. I just think that there were a lot of elements that, combined, created a lot of destruction—and a lot of good things as well."

Doris said she has gained something from every misfortune and mistake that has helped her in the philanthropic work she's doing now. "I look at my life story as everything that happened to me—when you take it as a whole of where I am today—whether it was sad or embarrassing or tragic or worrisome in the past, has been invaluable to me today because I learned lessons all along the way."

For the first sixty-eight years of her life, whoever was to blame, not much had gone right for Doris, despite being blessed with beauty, brains and charisma. Her life could be summed up by the classic Mr. T line in *Rocky III*. "My prediction?" the character, "Clubber" Lang, said before a fight. "Pain!"

But that was about to change. Because no matter how hard she was hit, she refused to stay down. Her stubbornness was about to pay off for thousands of people who needed a break themselves.

Discovering Dodo

Alex's first memory of his grandmother involves a wedding. He was four years old. "I had a couple of cousins—twin girls—who really tormented the hell out of me, at that wedding in particular." They had taken away young Alex's *Star Wars* action figures. "*Star Wars* was important to me back then," in part because Doris had taken him to see one of the films. "My grandmother was trying to console me and tell me that one day I was going to be bigger than those girls." That he would: eventually he would grow to six-foot-six and become a backup lineman as a non-scholarship walk-on for the University of North Carolina Tar Heels football team.

The wedding was also difficult for Doris. She was fifty-five and thrice divorced. She was still an attractive woman, but she didn't feel like one. Her mother's words were still rattling around in her head, she'd had terrible luck with men; and now here she was sitting through a wedding reception, at which no one had asked her to dance and only one adult talked to her. So Alex was clinging to her and she was clinging to him. That evening sent her into a period of depression, and she might not have made it through without her grandson.

Alex's childhood as a whole was hellish. He believes that both of his parents, Christopher Rozek and Robin Wood, suffer from mental illness. He says his father, a brilliant lawyer who had gone to Oxford and gotten a law degree at Duke University, developed a prescription drug problem, sending his family into a downward spiral that never seemed to end. After his parents divorced, Robin, who was living in Washington, moved to Fredericksburg, Virginia, about forty-five miles south on Interstate 95.

There was a custody fight. After half a dozen custody hearings, Robin finally gave up because she didn't feel she could win against her ex-husband, a talented lawyer when he wasn't high on drugs. Alex said Christopher began poisoning his mind against Doris, whom Alex continues to call "Dodo" to this day, saying she was a bad person and responsible for splitting up the family. For years as a boy, Alex had steered clear of Doris.

By age eight, Alex had decided he wanted to live with his father. "My father created this image of Dodo as evil," Alex said. "My father made it all 'You stay with me because your mom and Doris are evil. I'm the good parent.'" For five years, he had virtually nothing to do with his mother and grandmother. This was agonizing for both Robin and Doris.

But as Alex entered his teens, he started thinking for himself. "You get older and you figure out that's not the case," he said. "I started seeing a lot of lies. I talked to my mom on the phone and thought, 'She's not so bad. She's not a bad mother.'"

Entering a phase of teenage rebellion gave him a healthy outlook in spite of the chaos swirling around him. "A lot of kids rebel against being normal," he explained. "I rebelled to be normal. I asked to have what a lot of kids escaped from. I rebelled against the odd living situation with my dad. My father never let me have any friends. He wanted me to stay home with him on the weekends. My mom encouraged me to have friends. When I escaped the bizarre world with my dad, it was normal with my mom, what I'd always wanted."

After Alex's sophomore year of high school, he decided he wanted to live with his mother, "simply because I didn't want to live with him." He spent the summer in Boulder, Colorado, with his grandfather, Edward Rozek, who backed his decision to live with Robin. Alex and his mother moved into Doris' Mary Washington Square townhouse.

Alex had lived in a nearly unfurnished shell of a home with his father in Washington, never even having a bed. He'd slept on a futon in his father's room. The house was rarely well-stocked with food. Then, when he moved in with his mother in Fredericksburg, he walked into the house and couldn't believe it. There were pictures hanging on the wall. There was a couch. There was a dining room table.

"I'd been living a squatter's life for years," he said. "I remember thinking that the house in Fredericksburg was a haven, a sanctuary." After that, he cut off contact with his father. "That was the best thing I ever did," he said. "I made a bad choice when I was eight." Of Robin, he said, "She was a great mom." She drove him to the train station every day in Fredericksburg, so he could continue to attend Gonzaga High School in Washington.

And he reestablished his connection with his grandmother. When he was younger, Tuesdays had been pizza day with Dodo. And she had taken him to Hershey Park, where they made a game of "stealing" Hershey's Kisses. The candy was really free, but they would pretend it wasn't. Alex would stuff as many Kisses as he could into his clothes. Then they'd go back to the hotel, spread them on the floor, count them and laugh.

She also took him to the Amish country. "We went on a lot of adventures," he said. As they got to know each other again, the adventures resumed. Doris explained that she prefers giving grandchildren experiences rather than gifts.

When Alex was a young boy, he loved to go for rides with Doris. "Dodo had this Mercedes and we were driving on I-95, and I got her to drive over 100 miles an hour," he said. "I kept saying, 'Do it, do it, do it!'" Finally, Doris said, "Make sure there aren't any cops around," and floored the accelerator until the needle on the speedometer passed 100. Then she slowed down, and nervously made Alex swear he would never tell anyone. Of course, as soon as he got home, he delightedly told everyone.

When he moved to Fredericksburg to live with his mother, he didn't immediately embrace Doris. "I started off slow," he said. "I was apprehensive. I slowly observed and discovered my mom and my grandmother weren't evil people out to get me. It was quite the opposite."

For Doris it was a second chance. Like many grandparents, she got along better with her grandchildren than with their parents. In this case, Alex had brought her joy when he was a young child—then that happiness had been ripped away. It seemed the same old pattern in her life was continuing, as if on a loop. When he came back into her life, "I can hardly describe how wonderful it was," she said. "It almost seemed unreal to me that there'd be a happy ending. I was overjoyed. It had been a long time and it had also been a very sad time." Now she believes the same thing may be happening with Graham, Sydney's seventeen-year-old son who lives in Greenville, South Carolina. "It's just pure light," she said.

Alex almost bumped into his father jogging in Washington one day. Alex said Christopher saw him coming, pretended he didn't, and turned his head the other way to avoid speaking. The two brushed shoulders as Alex jogged past, but didn't acknowledge each other. It was just as well. "Every hour I spent trying to help my dad was an hour that could be spent trying to help my mom. She really deserves it. She's a good person."

Of Doris, Alex said, "How could anyone have more impact on my life? Literally, I think I have Dodo to thank for my wife."

In 2005, Doris and her friend Carolyn Firestone decided to fix Alex up on a date with Carolyn's great-niece, Sarah Gibbs "Mimi" Krueger. Alex lived in Washington and she was in New York. The two hit it off.

Then, in 2009, Alex proposed to Mimi in front of 35,000 people at the Berkshire Hathaway shareholders' meeting at the Quest Center in Omaha.

Reporter Bill Freehling of Fredericksburg's *Free Lance-Star* newspaper, who also writes a blog about Warren Buffett, described the proposal this way:

As the meeting drew to a close, Freehling wrote that Alex stood up and, *asked Warren Buffett what people could do to improve the U.S. economy. Buffett, showing no evidence that he knew Rozek, answered that it would be important to increase the number of households.*

Earlier in the meeting Buffett had explained that household formations are critical to soaking up the excess number of homes on the market. That in turn would stabilize the housing market and the broader economy.

Buffett, still not tipping his hand, then asked Rozek if the answer gave him any ideas.

Rozek, a 30-year-old who lives in Boston but spends a good amount of time in Fredericksburg, then turned to his girlfriend, got on his knees, told her she was his best friend, and proposed.

She said yes.

Buffett then revealed to the crowd that Rozek is his sister's grandson. The moment brought cheers from the crowd and ended the meeting on an upbeat note. Rozek said he came up with the idea about a month ago. He pitched it to Buffett by e-mail; Buffett liked the idea and thought it would be a good way to end the meeting.

Buffett told Rozek to ask a simple question about the economy right at 3 P.M. as the meeting was ending, and said he'd take it from there. "He's a showman," Rozek said.

Rozek said Krueger had no idea it was coming.

"It was fun," Alex said. Doris was elated. Convinced they were a perfect match, she was eager to see the two marry.

Doris and Alexander at her niece Susie's wedding to Alan Greenberg in New York City. No one asked Doris to dance.

WARREN ASKS FOR HELP

$oris calls August 30, 1930, "the luckiest day of my life." She was two years old when her brother Warren was born. When she says that now, she's making a tongue-in-cheek reference to the fact that his unparalleled genius as an investor has made her wealthy. But she clearly felt the same way before he could add two plus two.

But long before Warren's magic with money would take care of her, she took care of him. Not long ago, Warren gave her an inscribed photo showing a two-year-old Doris wearing a big bow in her hair, with her arm around a roly-poly baby, both smiling broadly.

Warren said his big sister's caring and giving nature was evident even before he learned to walk: "Doris always took care of me. My own empathy was self-centered. She was an older sister who looked after her brother to a great degree. And sometimes I needed a lot of looking after."

When they were young, she would hold his hand on the way to catch the streetcar to school, then bring him home on the same day. "He was easy to care for and love and play with," Doris said. "The amazing part is, here he is, the most powerful person in the world, and I still feel that way about him when it comes to some imagined slight or somebody taking a potshot at him."

Both Warren and Doris know all too well that money doesn't make one invulnerable. "He's had his [problems], too—we both have—when we were growing up at home, and later when we went out to have our lives."

They've both lived unconventional lives, and that can lead to isolation and even occasional derision. Doris has divorced four times—three of those during an era when divorce equaled disgrace.

Warren's beloved wife Susie left him to pursue a singing career, which broke his heart, even though they never divorced. Susie then introduced him to Astrid Marks, who moved in with Warren and took care of him. The relationship was so cordial that they spent the holidays together and signed Christmas cards "from Susie, Warren and Astrid." He then married Astrid after Susie died of cancer at age seventy-two in 2004.

"Susie left him and went to California," Doris said. "And he offered to go, and she said that wasn't what she wanted. He was as happy as a clam until that. That was a catastrophe to him. And I know how he felt when she died."

But she doesn't believe Warren has experienced people who attempt to take advantage of him to the degree that she has. "I don't think he's ever been double-crossed—it'd be pretty hard to do that."

Neither Warren nor Doris has spent much time in adulthood worrying about what the world thinks of them, either in their personal lives or their work. "I think she and I do things according to what makes sense to us and we don't pay much attention to the rest of the world," Warren said. "We both have that in common. We got that from our dad. Neither one of us is going to be conventional in the many things that we do—including philanthropy.

Warren with his wife Susie at his 50th birthday party in New York City.

"She's unconventional in a different way than I am," he said. "The world can handle conventionality . . . sometimes it doesn't handle unconventionality perfectly. I don't have any problem with that. Doris doesn't have any problem with that. My dad didn't have any problem with that. That's just not a factor."

Susie's death radically changed Warren's plans to give away his wealth to charity.

The Seattle Times reported that, Buffett had been expected to leave most of his wealth to the Susan Thompson Buffett Foundation, begun by him and his wife. It has given millions to hospitals, universities and teachers, as well as to Planned Parenthood. . . .

Instead, the wealth will be split among five foundations: the Gates Foundation, the Susan Thompson Buffett Foundation and three others in which Buffett's three children are involved. They support various issues like the environment, nuclear non-proliferation and education.

Buffett told Fortune *magazine his wife's death influenced his decision to start giving his money away now, and that he was impressed with the work of Bill and Melinda Gates. And he decided it would be easier to give to a large foundation instead of trying to expand his own foundation.*

"I always thought Susie would outlive me," Warren said. She was younger and women tend to live longer. And she was healthy. "I'd compound the wealth and she'd direct it largely after my death. We did some of that before, but not to this scale."

When Susie died first, Warren needed to come up with a sensible way of dispensing a huge amount of money for philanthropic use. "Susie and I'd always felt that all the proceeds from Berkshire were going to go to charity. I'd never sold a share and she'd never sold a share."

Even though his investment decisions have made billions for Berkshire Hathaway shareholders, Warren accepts an annual salary of only a $100,000. "So all of it—Berkshire—was going to go to charity," he said. But Warren knew that when Susie died, he had to find someone else to handle the distribution of the great wealth he has amassed. His thinking about philanthropy was not going to become more incisive from age seventy-four to eighty-four to ninety-four. "I'd seen people lose their faculties, particularly when you get up into that range. So I decided I should do it promptly. I should figure out what was the most rational way to essentially do the most good. That would not involve me quitting Berkshire and going to work at [philanthropy]. I wouldn't have been that good. And I was older. And I had such an obvious choice in that."

Warren had become close friends with Microsoft founder Bill Gates, who is twenty-five years younger. "Here you had two people [Bill and Melinda Gates] who were much younger. Who were very bright. Who had the same objective, basically, that I did, in terms of philanthropy. And who were doing it big time with their own money, who had a lot of experience and were going to spend virtually full-time at it in their future lives, for decades. And they were already scaled up. So they were an obvious choice. So were the other four foundations that I left it to, that I made arrangements with. But they couldn't operate on the same scale. I'm very pleased about not only how Gates is handling things, but how the other four are as well."

Holding onto his Berkshire Hathaway shares as long as possible and working hard to build their value, then having someone else choose charities where it could do the most good was a no-brainer to him. "People came to me fifty years ago and said, 'You're better at investing money than I am,' so they turned their money over to me," Warren said. "And I said to these people, 'You're going to be better at giving it away than I would be. So I'm going to hand it over to you now.' So far it's working perfectly."

Warren thought about giving billions to Doris' Sunshine Lady Foundation, but decided against that for a very logical reason. "If Doris was fifty, I might well have done something very big with her," Warren said. "But she's got the same problem I've got. We've got a limited span of how long we can do this."

When Warren announced in 2007 that he would give eighty-three percent of his wealth, at that time about $31 billion, to the Bill & Melinda Gates Foundation, at a rate of five percent a year, it was the biggest charitable gift in history. And it caught the attention of the whole world. Thousands of letters began piling up asking Warren for help. Since Doris specialized in "retail" philanthropy, he asked her if she would take on the letters he was receiving. He scribbled a note, "Do you want to take these?" on the back of a sample letter and sent it to Doris. She was thrilled to be asked and was eager to do it.

"He does philanthropy in a really big way—and is one of the smartest [philanthropists]," Doris said of Warren.

She called a member of her Foundation board, Diane Grimsley, and could almost hear her pursing her lips. "I don't think that's a very good idea," Diane said, because the Foundation was already handling so many of its own letters pleading for help. "But I thought it was a terrific opportunity, and so I overrode her and she'll never get over that," Doris said, laughing. She called Warren's office the next morning and said yes.

He later promised to keep money flowing to her Foundation for use in response to the letters that had been addressed to him.

Doris set up reading groups from Camden, Maine, which is a short distance from her home in Rockport—and then all the way down to Wilmington, North Carolina. She sent them each 200 or so letters and they were to rank them. She said not to do anything with letters from foreign countries "because I didn't know anything about foreign currency and banking and all that, and because we couldn't check on the people. But that was hard because they were the most pathetic of all the letters. It was really hard to ignore them, but I really didn't know any other way to do it."

In any case, eighty percent were from the U.S. "Obviously, there were some pretty big problems right here in this country," Doris said. "We put them aside and were to mark them 'urgent' with a big 'U,' and we tried to get to those first. And we did, but by the time we even got through those, three people had died. So we weren't kidding around."

Maine Sunshine Lady Foundation staff: Buffy Krause, Kathleen Oliver, Poesy Barlow, Vicki Hamlin, Doris, Noni Campbell, Nancie Burton, Valerie Allis.

These were about critical needs. And time was short for those who were writing—people with cancer, children who were very ill, families facing foreclosures.

Doris started right away. She sat down on the couch with a phone by her side, and started going through the letters and calling. People were amazed that they got any kind of response from their letters. And then when they heard that it was Warren's sister, they were in a state of disbelief.

"And that was nice because they really felt like somebody cared about them," Doris said. So we talked and I would ask all kinds of questions, and they would tell me the whole story. Nobody held back. I was really amazed. I practically never ran into that. They were just really happy to talk to somebody." Eventually, she had piles in various stages around her chair. She had to do something about this.

"I got four friends—new friends, actually—women in their fifties, to help me with it in Maine. I picked that age group because they're old enough to know something and have had some life experience. I find that they have more empathy as they get older, and they were bright and they caught on and they did a lot of research on such things as reverse mortgages, credit counseling. One woman even had a bad tooth, and one of the girls told her how to tie a string around it and onto a door, and she got her tooth pulled out. So no detail is too small for us."

It's grueling, detail-oriented work, but Doris' group loves it. "I don't know a woman that doesn't like to give advice. So we gave out as much advice as money, I suppose."

In 2007, the CBS Morning Show did a segment on Warren and Doris teaming up, and anchor Harry Smith described Doris and each member of her crew sifting through the letters as combination "social worker, private detective and life coach."

There are some letters from people who are simply greedy, and some from the mentally ill. "We get letters from 'the Virgin Mary,' who, by the way, is not a very nice person," Doris said with a chuckle. She was expecting more from those who thought, "Well, I'll apply and get my million or two." But the true stories from real people—"They've blown me away. We've seen humanity in a different way."

Still, Doris doesn't like foundations that are loosey-goosey when giving away what she refers to as "OPM" or "other people's money," and she's certainly not going to be that way with Warren's. She makes sure people really need the help; that they can't fix their problems on their own; and then she's not extravagant in doling out the money. She's compassionate, but she's also tough and business-minded. One woman who spoke to Doris wrote a second time to Warren, saying, "Please help me, but don't send me back to your sister again."

The CBS Morning Show noted that one man wrote to Warren to say: "I don't know what's wrong, but I'm forty-one years old and have nothing to show for it. And Mr. Buffett, if you'd send $10 million, it would make all the difference in the world." That drew gales of laughter from Doris' "girls."

But then there are letters from people like Kathleen O'Neill, a single mother who was unable to work because of illness, and who desperately needed a car. She tearfully told CBS that Doris had called her personally: "Doris doesn't make you feel bad. She doesn't make you feel beneath her. She doesn't make you feel like you're poor. She makes you feel like you're her friend."

Doris' sister Bertie was also moved. "This is a culmination to a life that hasn't been easy," she said, starting to cry. "This work that she's doing now, that my brother's made possible, is a real blessing, a real state of grace in a sense."

It's Just Bad Luck

The thousands of letters to Warren, that Doris and the Sunshine Lady Foundation are handling, usually start out much the same way.

"They say, 'I've seen you on TV and you have a kind face,'" Doris said. Or, 'I've heard what you're doing and you must be a very nice man.' Or things like, 'I think that some of this money could be spent on people in the United States.' And some would say, 'I've called the Gates Foundation and they don't help poor people.' I'm sure Bill would love hearing that! And they've 'tried all sorts of agencies' in their hometown and they aren't getting any help.

"Then they describe their circumstances in great detail. And the final paragraph, about two-thirds of the time, if not more, goes something like this: 'I'm sure you're getting dozens of letters and if you're reading this, I'm honored. If you have people who need money more than we do who are in worse situations and we don't get any money, we understand. And we'll pray for you and your family every night for the rest of our lives.'" Doris is continually astonished by that.

"I became convinced more than ever that there are some really decent people in this country who just haven't had it as good as some other people have. I also realized that poor people get terrible medical help and get very bad legal advice, too. They don't have the money. In some cases, we could rectify that."

There was a man in Iowa who was born with a rare condition that made it difficult to eat and talk, Doris said. He had no health insurance and the cost for care was $6,000 a treatment. He was a gardener and made little money. Doris called the Mayo Clinic. In ten minutes, she had a call back from the head of neurology and he said, "Oh, I did all my post-grad work in this. There are only 100,000 cases in the world."

"How in the world do you get this?" Doris asked the doctor, who replied, "It's just bad luck."

"So much of it is just bad luck," she said. "That happened before he was born and that man would be stuck with that his whole life. So, that was one thing we could do to help."

The SLF's Buffy Krause received a letter from a grandmother whose grandchildren perished in a fire. "I think they were ages one, two and three," Doris said. "And all she wanted was a gravestone. That meant everything in the world to her. And we were able to do that."

Another man had a false eye he had used for thirty years. It wasn't the right size anymore and he offered to send it to the Sunshine Lady Foundation, "which we declined," Doris said with a laugh. "But he got his new eye."

A mother in Tennessee noticed a spot on her eleven-year-old daughter's eye that didn't go away. The mother was a waitress with no health insurance, divorced, and raising three children on her own. A biopsy indicated it was a fungal disease. The doctor said there had been thirty-two such cases in Thailand and three in the U.S. The fungus had spread its tentacles and there were surgeries needed on both eyes, her nose, then her brain. Meanwhile, her mother was working the night shift at a restaurant so she could spend her days at the hospital. The girl survived the ordeal, and the SLF helped with her mother's bills. "I'd certainly call that case bad luck," Doris said. "There are thousands out there."

Then there are retired elderly people who run into unexpected expenses and can't make it. Social Security barely covers their house payments, leaving little or nothing to live on. She helped one elderly couple in Kentucky buy the first home they ever owned. Or they've had a major illness and found themselves in debt. Sometimes they've put it on credit cards. "With a hospital, sometimes they'll take ten dollars a month—or whatever—or sometimes they'll even write it off," Doris said. "But with a credit card, you're stuck. They have bills that in a million years they could never pay. Many of them have gone into bankruptcy. We really try not to give handouts in every case. We like to give hand ups. If it's handouts, that's usually the result of bad choices. Not that we all haven't made bad choices. But when people make one bad choice after another, sometimes we can't help."

Sometimes the Sunshine Lady Foundation simply gives advice. "And with our combined knowledge and experience, we think we give pretty good advice." Some recipients think so too. One woman wrote Doris and said, "You could be the mother of us all." Doris may seem motherly to some, but she takes a businesslike approach to her philanthropy.

"We always check everything," she said. Initially, too much of the business between the Sunshine Lady Foundation and those seeking help was being done by long, tedious phone calls. "This phone call business was going on twelve hours a day. I was wearing out my sofa just sitting there and gaining weight," Doris said. "So we devised a letter we send to everybody who falls in our category, and we ask them to send us right away proof of their income and proof of their medical condition, if that's their problem."

The Sunshine Lady Foundation definitely checks things out. Sometimes the Sunshine Lady herself does. In 2008, when a young man applied for a scholarship, he divulged that he had recently inherited $100,000 from his father, whom he had not seen in years. The young man explained that his father stated in his will that the money should be used to start a business, and asked if he could still interview for a scholarship so he wouldn't be going against his father's wishes. He said he and his mother were living in a small trailer and had no money. Minutes before Doris was to meet him in North Carolina for the interview, she hopped into a friend's car and roared across town to check out the address to make sure there really was a trailer there. When she confirmed that, the wheels of the car squealed as she made a quick U-turn and raced back to the house where they were to meet. She got there just in time to shake his hand as he came in. The young man got his scholarship.

She prefers to do things in a more orderly way, but wasn't afraid to get her hands dirty in that situation—when she was eighty.

"If it's a house [in jeopardy], we ask for all the information regarding that. That cuts through a lot of time. You can get a whole lot more efficient if we give them a deadline, and we always hand-write something on the letter; and we hear back from almost all of them. Which also says that they're not faking it. But still, it's just an endless amount of time because it just has to be."

She adores Warren, but she's businesslike with him, too, in a tongue-in-cheek way, when it comes to the work that involves helping with the letters he receives. "After I talked to my brother and said, 'Yeah, we'll take them,' about six months later, I was talking to him because he'd just gotten married and I was congratulating him. I said 'Yeah, we got the letters, but there was no money that came along with it.' Which I thought was a little sisterly joke. I really did. Mitty and I already talked about how much money we were going to take out of the Foundation. But he just sort of gave a little nervous laugh, and the very next day I got a letter from him that he'd already sent before we talked. In it he said that he was going to send me $5 million to accomplish this, and if I needed more I could have it. We were overcome by that."

As fulfilling as the work is, some question her motivation. "I had someone say to me once, in sort of a negative tone, 'I think anytime someone gives something to somebody, they're getting something for it,' meaning they're really doing it to make themselves feel good, not to help others. It wasn't said in a nice way. There was a real message there. I was taken aback by it."

Mitty Beal, Doris' executive director, doesn't have to think about that question: "Well, I don't ever remember wondering why she did it. I just accepted that she did. The way she does it seems so natural. There's nothing pretentious about it. There's nothing bureaucratic about it. It never enters Doris' mind—there isn't a reason *not* to do it. Not to be generous. She has everything she wants. She has modest desires. She has two really nice houses and a decent car, and she doesn't really want a lot. So she has a lot of money, and figures, 'Why not?'

"I think that's her motto. People say why do you do it, and she says, 'Why not?' and that makes a lot of sense," Mitty said. But Doris has really thought about the question.

"I thought I'm not earning Brownie points for heaven and I'm not doing it for publicity, because that really just back-fires on you. So what am I getting out of it? What's my payoff? It wasn't hard to figure out. And it wasn't a bad thing.

"My payoff is the constant joy that I have thinking somebody's life is a little better," Doris said. "They have hope. They have a feeling that they matter to someone. They're not disposable. That for once in their life, they have good luck, not bad luck. Like nothing's gone right for them, and they have a day they can look back on and think there was a day when I got a phone call or received a check or I talked to another human being who was interested in what was going on in my life.

"I don't feel better than anyone else," she said. "I feel like I've taken advantage of my circumstances, which changed midlife. And that's enough for me. I would wish that other people can experience it, because I think it's the headiest thing in the world." Buying another home or a new car or jewelry can't create the same kind of feeling. "It certainly beats—it definitely beats—material possessions," she said. "If you have any sense of fairness, the hands we're dealt vary from one to another—we really don't have anything to say about it. It's also made me realize that in my own life, my problems have been minor compared to others, because some people have had it really, really hard."

She does receive some material payoffs, though. She walks across her living room in Fredericksburg, and picks up a painstakingly hand-carved wooden car about the size of a shoebox and it fits in her lap when she sits down. "This is a Model T—a Ford Model T, 1921. It was sent to me by a family in Louisiana. I can't remember what we did for them. But they sat down as a family and decided they wanted to send me something that meant something to them, which is pretty overwhelming. Turns out the car is made by Michael—the husband, he made it for his father—because this was a replica of the first car his father ever rode in. I found that very touching."

And there are pictures. And fudge at Christmastime, "Which," she says with a chuckle, "I do not share." And then there are the letters. "They write from the heart. So I would say the letters are the most wonderful opportunity to connect with people who really need it."

One of the biggest rewards is the bond she's formed with the women she works with in the Sunshine Lady Foundation. "How could another group do this? I say nobody could because it takes all the right people and I've got all of them. We have fifteen people. How could another group really do this? I have all the best people who are all part of the Sunshine Lady Foundation—everyone is a jewel."

Every community organization, she said, should have a discretionary fund for the unexpected things that come up. Some do. But more should. "We have them at the University of Virginia's Children's Hospital; we have them at any number of safe houses for battered women. We put them in their hands and say use it for whatever you need it for—for whatever's necessary. In safe houses, they may use them to retool the locks. They may have to take a plane to go somewhere or rent a truck to haul their belongings. There are a variety of needs that come up for women who show up there."

For schools, she said, "It's for when you don't have a dress for the prom or when you can't rent a tux, or some of those things that may break your life at that point."

If every big foundation could have a small division, with a special fund with one person in charge of it, deserving individuals who've had bad luck can be helped. "You certainly couldn't do it on a national level; before you know it you'd have a big bureaucracy," Doris said. She's suspicious of large foundations.

"Everybody wants to build an empire. That's why we try to stick to working with outfits that have a smaller budget, because once it goes over a certain point it's for a new building or more hires, and you just get caught up in it, and then have a bureaucracy."

Once Doris spoke to a group of philanthropists, "a mass meeting of philanthropists or people thinking about becoming one. It was depressing for me. The majority of the conversation was 'How can we save on taxes? How can we set up our grandchildren so they can be in charge of these things we set up?' I heard very little about philanthropy."

When the event wrapped up with a discussion led by Bill Moyers, the only organization that was mentioned by name was the Sunshine Lady Foundation. They concluded that Doris' Foundation signified what philanthropy was supposed to be about—getting help to people who really need help. And the SLF was praised for doing its work with only five percent overhead and for being bureaucracy-free. "So I floated out of there, and I was not fit to be lived with for three weeks," Doris said.

Instead of building an empire, Doris rents two modest offices for her Foundation. "The girls will call me up really excited and say, 'We figured out how to send this mailing out for twenty-two cents a piece instead of thirty-two,' or something like that. And I think that's really terrific."

Once, when a woman was about to be evicted from her home because of debt, Doris agreed to buy her a new place to live, but said it would be a mobile home—and a used one at that. So Doris found one in the classified ads, hopped into her car and drove alone into a bad section of town. She realized she was wearing a multiple-carat diamond ring, and figured it wouldn't be a good idea to be flashing it around all alone. So she dropped it into the console compartment between the front seats. She heard a clinking sound: the car had to be taken apart to find the ring.

Was the ring insured? No. Did she insure it after that scare? No, she said, because making those payments over time, you might as well buy a new ring.

She doesn't liquidate any more Berkshire Hathaway stock than is necessary each year because Warren does such a good job of increasing its value. At the end of one year, when Mitty finished doing the Sunshine Lady Foundation's nonprofit paperwork, there was ninety-nine cents left on the books.

"As they need money, I transfer the stock," Doris said. "We have the right spirit. I'm not a miser about it." To the contrary, she's completely serious about wanting to give away all her money by the time her life ends. She just wants to be judicious enough so that it does the most good possible for the largest number of people.

"I'm in such a hurry to get this out that I told each of the board members they can spend a million dollars. We'd like to give away a million a month because it's a lot of money and I'm a lot of years old. So we really have to add zip to it. They're all working away on things. Now that doesn't mean they can give it to some goofy cause. The same rules apply whether it's ten dollars or a million dollars."

Doris loves helping children, because in many cases they have no advocates. "We love education because it's really the only way out of poverty," she said. "We don't limit it to that, but it's our top priority."

"We love to help women who've been battered, who have no self-esteem, no confidence," she said. "We've had admirable success with our Women's Independence Scholarship Program (WISP) for a decade now. Two graduates of the WISP program have gone on to the Wharton School of Business after once being afraid to walk out on abusive husbands and boyfriends." There are typically 500 women enrolled in the program at any time. And Doris has given WISP a $30 million endowment so it will continue long after she's gone.

WISP scholars go to the school of their choice. Tuition and books account for only about a fourth of the funds they are allotted, because they need so much help with other things, including child care, rent and transportation. And most battered women receive little or no medical care.

"We've had a few of them die," Doris said. "So they need to see a doctor right away. And they often need dental care from being punched and having their teeth knocked out. That runs about $3 million a year. We try to keep up with them. We have a woman who calls them every year to make sure they're OK. We have to do it carefully—it's arduous. There are children and bills, and someone may be stalking them, and they may not be in good health, the children may not be in good health, so they really need a lot of help." They come to Doris through safe houses from all over the country.

Upon graduation from college, most WISP scholars choose to go into the field of social services. Many go back into domestic-violence work because they know what it's like to be a victim. "We've helped build a lot of shelters and we feel good about that because this problem isn't going away." Doris is concerned about children learning to be abusive from their fathers, and she wants to get them

Tammy Hartley, Diane Grimsley, Nancy Soward, Jill Large, and Doris announcing the establishment of WISP, Inc. as a separate entity from the Sunshine Lady Foundation, after a $30 million grant from Doris ensured it would continue its work of educating battered women after she is gone. 2009.

out of that environment as quickly as possible so that it isn't passed on from one generation to the next.

She has a letter from a woman who said she's studying to become a nurse, and whose daughter told her, "Well, one day I'm going to be your boss, because I'm going to be a doctor." So it raises expectations in families and creates an entirely different view of school. Another letter from a WISP scholarship recipient said: "A year ago today, I was in the hospital with fifty-one fractures in my face. My husband came at me with a crowbar. Today I'm sitting here with my children; we're all doing our homework. I'm enrolled in college and our life has taken a big upward swing." One woman from Doris' hometown of Omaha wrote that her husband kept her inside the house with the shades drawn for ten years, and now she's finally out.

WISP came about early in the game because Doris decided she wanted to reward women who had been in the domestic-violence business a long time. They often went into it because they'd been battered and survived and wanted to help other women. Then Doris started sending children from low-income families to camp. The first group of children was being taken to the mountains, and one asked how she would know when she was in the mountains. "What's a mountain?" she asked.

Part of the initial purpose of the camps, aside from allowing children to escape oppressive poverty for a month, was to instill in them the idea of value in reaching out to others and helping them. "In everything we've ever done, and this was long before the book or movie came out, we have stressed that you have to pay it forward," Doris said. "We didn't call it that, but we said you had to do something good for someone later in your life when you're able to. That's how I got started."

The camps led to one of Doris' favorite letters: "Since I've been home, I've been helping around the house and doing what my mother tells me to do and helping other people," an eight-year-old boy wrote. "And I will continue to do kind things, even after you've gone to the Great Beyond." She laughs and says that's her best letter from a child—the Great Beyond Letter.

Next she decided to build a Boys & Girls Club in Morehead City, North Carolina. She'd been on the board of the Boys & Girls Club in nearby Beaufort. She made a substantial challenge grant and they agreed. But the board in Morehead City put no money into the project, while she was putting in $500,000. Doris equates that to buying stock in a company in which the board owns no shares. But she formed allegiances and finally got it built. It has an annual budget of $750,000, which is substantial for a small town.

Doris said it was the first time she had encountered racism in her charitable work. "Someone visited a lawyer there to ask for a contribution, and he said, 'I ain't givin' a dime to babysit no [N-words].'"

"'Why would you help a black child?' That happened, for sure," said Diane Grimsley. "The first time Doris tried to do something major, it was a million-dollar grant to the community foundation, and they turned her down because it would have required an audit and 100 percent of the board needed to be involved. They were terribly threatened. 'Who is this lady?' 'She's not from here.'"

SLF Scholarship Coordinator Mary Ellen Box said much of the resistance came from "good old boy" types who also resented the idea of a woman trying to tell them what to do. But the resistance gradually melted away.

"Now, when she comes to Morehead City, it's like the queen has come home," Diane said. "They gave her an award that usually brings out a crowd of ten or fifteen people.

Doris drew 300. And they went around the room, one by one, standing up and saying what the Sunshine Lady had done for them. "She dragged that board from kicking-and-screaming to really jumping on the bandwagon," Grimsley said. "Those who felt threatened are big fans now."

Doris learned a lot from that Boys & Girls Club experience—how to write a contract, a proposal, how to write an agreement. "One thing you have to know when you go into this business is that it's a business," Doris said. "It's a big business if you have a lot of money and you go into it with a lot of heart."

When Doris offered $2.5 million for a Boys & Girls Club in Fredericksburg, there was a disagreement over the best site. She wanted it in a spot easily accessible from several low-income neighborhoods. CLAY JONES POLITICAL CARTOON REPRINTED WITH PERMISSION FROM THE FREE LANCE-STAR.

Mental Illness and the Buffetts

In 2008, the city of Fredericksburg was conducting a sweep of a wooded area where homeless people had set up tents, gathering up the tents and belongings of the homeless and burning them. It was part of an effort to force the homeless into shelters or leaving the city. Studies show that as many of fifty percent of the homeless end up in that position because they are mentally ill and cannot hold a job; or, in some cases, even function at the most basic level of society.

Rebecca Currie, a member of the Sunshine Lady Foundation board and a psychiatric nursing instructor at Career Training Solutions, a private nursing school in Fredericksburg, said she believes the percentage is much higher than that. "A lot of the homeless are alcoholics or drug addicts," she said. "Mentally ill people tend to not have family, do not have friends, but they can be in a group socially with drugs or alcohol—and they use drugs or alcohol to self-medicate." Many of those in that group may never have been diagnosed with mental illness, but it has ruined their lives without them realizing it. Therapy and medication could help.

Some who have been diagnosed, Currie elaborated, "self-medicate with drugs or alcohol because they can't afford the medicine or they believe the CIA is watching them. They're not going to go stand in line and pay $500 for their medicine. They just can't function well enough to do that and there is usually no medication provided. Sometimes we find a source that will provide medication."

There were only about thirty beds at Snowden, a mental health facility in Fredericksburg, and people were being released or turned away because of a shortage of space, Currie said. "They're full. Crisis stabilization is full, or the person doesn't want to go to the homeless shelter. The shelter has a lot of rules, and the shelter helps a lot of people, but the shelter is not going to take the alcoholics or the drug addicts. I'll call the Baptist church and they'll send a tent," she said. "My students will bring in food that's nonperishable. We'll pack a backpack and send them out with as much as we possibly can." But to some people, that's like feeding feral cats, so the city made its sweep.

Doris met with Ron Branscome, director of the Rappahannock Area Community Services Board, and offered to donate $2 million to renovate and expand its center for mentally ill people in crisis, and also build a beautiful, twelve-bedroom Sunshine Lady House for Mental Health Wellness and Recovery in downtown Fredericksburg.

Amy Umble of *The Free Lance-Star* newspaper in Fredericksburg reported:

> *Many parents of adults with mental illnesses choked back tears at the grand opening. The house represents a safe place where their children could recover from crises. Patients receive up to 15 days of treatment including 24-hour supervision, art therapy, group sessions and counseling. The*

grant will also provide long-term housing in the form of apartments for eight adults with serious mental illnesses.

"I would feel sorry for them after hearing Rebecca tell me how they lived and how ill-treated they were," Doris said. "But that doesn't account for the amount of joy I had when I saw the building ready for the new occupants. Mental illness was a tragedy in my mother's life and my grandmother's, as it has been in mine. So I get an extra wallop out of that. A sense of you can't make up for the past, but you can do something to help other people. You can't do anything about the ones that are gone. That's the saddest thing."

Rebecca said it meant a lot that the Sunshine Lady was standing up for this powerless group. "It's easy to put these people aside because no one's going to advocate for them. Maybe their families if they haven't made their families so jaded and worn out from their disease. It's terrible. They're just sort of on their own. They're not going to get in their car and go to Richmond and talk to the legislature. Who's going to do it? No one."

It's not the first time that Doris had made a major donation that could help the mentally ill. One she made in 2007 to the FRAXA Research Foundation could potentially have a huge impact. She offered a $500,000 challenge grant. The challenge led to 2,600 people donating $1.5 million, and the Sunshine Lady Foundation matched that, bringing the total generated by her initial challenge gift to $3.5 million. All of it was to be used for clinical trials and new research in an attempt to cure Fragile X, a genetic defect that was considered in 2010 "the most common inherited cause of intellectual impairment and the most common known genetic cause of autism." News reports had indicated a byproduct of the research could be more effective treatments for depression.

Doris made a point of telling *The Free Lance-Star* that there had been, "a lot of mental illness in my family."

Warren has acknowledged that the Buffett family has felt the sting of mental illness. Leila's mother was incapacitated by it. One of Leila's sisters committed suicide, and the other attempted it. "If you go back a generation or two generations there was a history of problems, and some of them were mental. But I wouldn't attribute any of that to my mother. She just was very tough in certain ways."

"My great-grandmother, Susan Watkins Barber, was in an insane asylum in the 1880s, the Nebraska State Mental Hospital, and my grandmother, Stella Barber Stahl, died there," Doris said.

Doris said Warren took legal action to have state records released about their grandmother, and that he learned "she had twenty-six electric shock treatments of the old variety."

"We know that depression very clearly runs in families," said David Fassler, a Burlington, Vermont psychiatrist and author of the book, *Help Me, I'm Sad: Recognizing, Treating and Preventing Childhood and Adolescent Depression*, and a member of the Board of Trustees of the American Psychiatric Association. "There's a very definite genetic component. If you have one or two parents with depression, you have a significantly higher risk of developing it. And if you have a parent, sibling or grandparent who committed suicide, you have a much greater risk of committing suicide yourself." He also said, "Someone who is depressed is going to have more problems, disappointments and traumas in their lives."

As Jonathan Alpert, a medical doctor and Ph.D. who has been Associate Director of the Depression Clinical and

The Buffett siblings and their spouses. STANDING (FROM LEFT TO RIGHT): Katie, Howard, Alice, Irma, Helen. SEATED (FROM LEFT TO RIGHT) Fred, Leila with Doris on her lap, Grandpa Ernest Buffett, Clarence with little George on his lap, George. 1930.

Leila at home with the kids in the family living room in Washington in 1944.

Research Program at Massachusetts General Hospital, and has taught at Harvard Medical School, said: "Sometimes people can be severely depressed even though they are the envy of their friends and neighbors. We see many people who are quite depressed even though they realize they have very good lives. They're on vacation, on the beach in Aruba, and everyone else is having a great time and they just wish they could die. That disparity makes it clear."

The fact that Warren and Doris Buffett are talking openly about mental illness and suicide in their family—associating the name Buffett, one of the most respected in the world, with those things—could help ease the stigma, said David Vaughn, president of the Rappahannock affiliate of the National Alliance on Mental Illness. "They're kind of coming out of the closet with their family illnesses—even some of their own illnesses, and now they've given back with this building, so it's a visible symbol. Here it is—in front of your face—you can see it."

The Girls

The key to success of the innovative approach of the Sunshine Lady Foundation is the fact that Doris assembled a small, disparate band of women with no experience in philanthropy, but with experience and skills that fit neatly together like a jigsaw puzzle. Through gut instinct, Doris jumped into projects other women were involved in to lend a hand. She quickly got to know them well enough to see that they were smart and dedicated, had good hearts, but were also tough and pragmatic.

After more than six decades of unfortunate choices in her personal life, her gut instincts started to work for her when she began the Foundation in 1996. They have been critical to both choosing people for the Foundation and to making the right choices in dealing with thousands in need, often one on one. Focusing on other people's problems, getting results and receiving heartfelt thanks from those she helped went a long way toward helping her set unhappy memories aside. And it turned her into a force of nature that wouldn't let up until good things happen.

"In a nutshell," her sister Bertie said, "Doris has always been very creative and is exceptionally good at leadership type roles—entrepreneurial—all of those things where you think of an idea, march forward with it and other people become attracted to it. The Sunshine Lady Foundation makes use of its people's best talents and it's a wonderful expression of her own talents. And it does a lot of good things for people."

Here are a few of the "girls" who work with Doris at the Sunshine Lady Foundation:

MITTY BEAL, *Executive Director,*
Sunshine Lady Foundation

"I was on the board of a little private school called The Tiller School. It was started in Beaufort, North Carolina, by a bunch of mostly Yankees that didn't want to send their kids to the local public school. So we started this little school and we were scrambling for money. Someone said to me, 'You ought to call Doris Buffett, she's Jimmy Buffett's sister, and I heard she gives away money.' So I called her, and introduced myself and told the story. I said, 'would you like to come over and see the school?' She said, 'Yes,' I asked, 'when?' and she said, 'I'll come right now.' So Doris jumped in her old Toyota van, came over, looked around the school, and made a generous grant on the spot."

Mitty, who lives in Philadelphia now, was so impressed that she wrote to Doris in the summer of 1997 and said, "If you ever need a hand, I would sure like to work for the Sunshine Lady." She called Doris and they went out to lunch. Doris said, "Well, I really don't have anything I need you to do, except I would really like to have help with my personal correspondence."

"So I said, 'OK, I could help you with that.' I had no idea what I would do, and then the next week there was a newspaper article that was picked up by the AP. After that it was in papers all over the country. It said, 'North

Carolina woman looking for places to give away money,' and people started to write, and they wrote and wrote and wrote. A lot of the letters said, 'I saw your ad in the paper,' so we called that 'Ad No. 1,' which created lots of employment for me. And that's how we started. I was thrown right into it."

It seemed that Mitty's involvement was meant to be. "I used to go over to her house every morning and we would go through the next batch of letters. She had loads of questions for lots of people. E-mail wasn't done then, so I had to call them all. It was exciting, but it was also very wearing. I was using the phone in my own house, I didn't have an office, and so people were calling all the time." When that died down a bit, Doris put her in charge of the Sunbeams. This kept her busy because there were about a hundred Sunbeams, and they were all selecting various projects."

Mitty said Doris' personal nature, her tendency to empathize with people she doesn't know, along with her own past, combined to make this work a natural thing for her. "I think it's ingrained. She's clearly had a lot of life experience, a lot of it very exciting and fun, and she's had a lot of challenges—personal challenges—with a lot of heartbreak. By nature she's an optimistic person and knows that she's making a difference in a lot of people's lives. And she is. People always say, 'What's her interest in domestic violence? Where's that come from? Was she ever physically abused?' And I say, 'Uh, no, she wasn't, she just identifies with people who have suffered.'"

When bad things happen in life, it causes most people to clutch tightly onto whatever they have. They feel insecure. They know how hard things can be and don't want to ever return to that point. As Vivien Leigh's Scarlett O'Hara says in Gone with the Wind, "As God is my witness,

I'll never be hungry again!" Like Scarlett, Doris refused to roll over. But instead of protecting herself, she's focused outward on the needs of others, even though that sometimes leaves her open to further disappointments.

"She's been through a lot in life," Mitty said, "yet she just keeps coming back and coming back. It's really inspiring. She just doesn't get defeated. The resilience is incredible. I love how on soap operas they get divorced, they kill people and then they come back to life, they lose their children, and that's how Doris is. She has a resilience that's unreal. And not everybody has that. Hardly anybody has that. I think it's just there. If you sliced her open you'd see it—it would have a specific color and it'd be marbled throughout. It's just there. It's in the genes. If I could wish for any characteristic for my daughter it'd be resilience. You need it. And you're really lucky if you have it."

Mitty said working for the Sunshine Lady Foundation has changed her: "I'm capable of being judgmental, and I've really cut back on that. Judging people for where they are in life and through all these people—encountering all these people who have written to us—I see that I've been extraordinarily lucky in my life, and I've learned by dealing with people who have had terrible lives through no fault of their own. We like to think that people are in bad situations because of their actions, because that excuses us our comfort and our good luck. I've come to realize I don't deserve my good luck, just like other people don't deserve their bad luck, and this has made me a much happier person.

"I'm so grateful for what I have. I'm fortunate to have good health, a wonderful family, a daughter who I love, great friends, and a wonderful job. And it's luck and timing. I started out lucky and I have—just luck. I haven't made a bunch of crummy decisions. I think that's luck too. And

I don't think I would've known that if I hadn't had the experience of working with the Sunshine Lady. I'm not so insulated or isolated as we tend to be in our little neighborhoods and our social strata. It's very easy to be ignorant of what's going on elsewhere."

She feels good about seeing Doris recognized in the media for her work. "Not just for her generosity, but for the very clever way that she's gone about setting up the Sunshine Lady Foundation. It's a very informal, low-cost structure that really works, and people who work for the Foundation love what they're doing. So she's been validated. After eighty years of thinking that she was the screw-up in the family, it turns out that maybe she isn't. And that's been wonderful to see. She never thought that other people would realize that this is a pretty efficient way of helping a lot of people."

But for many, it would be a double-edged sword. The more you help, the more attention you get and the more you feel that everyone wants something from you, and that people take advantage of you or are scamming you.

"I think it would feel that way for a type of person, and I think that Doris at times feels that people are after her money," Mitty said. "But she has such a huge personality and she's so much fun, that she knows that people would want her company whether she had any money to give away or not. She has charisma. She's tremendously interesting and vibrant and amusing. And she has money to give away, so that's one of the things you can ask for from her. But besides asking for money, you can ask for her company, her insights, her thoughts, her wisdom, and her fun. The money is just a part of the menu. For the people who really get to know her, it's the less important part. She hasn't had the money for all that long in terms of her whole life. She was certainly making friends long before the money—and good friends. Doris has lots of good friends that she's hung on to."

In 2004, Doris made Mitty executive director of the Foundation so she could be a stand-in for her and take some of the responsibility off her back. "In everything we've done," Mitty explained, "we've become more focused, a little bit more businesslike. The more we get to be known, the more demands increase, so we've had to develop consistent policies and approaches, otherwise we'll just be torn to bits by requests."

Still, other members of the Foundation laugh and say that when they get a difficult case, they stop and ask each other, "WWDD? What would Doris do?"

DIANE GRIMSLEY, *Vice President,*
Sunshine Lady Foundation board

Diane became close friends with Doris before she inherited the money she used to start the Sunshine Lady Foundation, then became a part of it, and watched Doris take her first steps as a philanthropist.

Diane oversees the Sunshine Lady Foundation's financial office and the scholarship program with Mary Ellen Box. She's also a member of the board of the Women's Independence Scholarship Program that assists battered women. WISP had just been broken off from the Sunshine Lady Foundation when Doris gave it a $30 million grant and made it a nonprofit. Since 1999, WISP has awarded more than $20 million in scholarships to more than 2,000 survivors. It has also awarded about 100 Counselor, Advocate and Support Staff scholarships to workers in the field of domestic violence.

Diane met Doris when she was running a program at the local hospital that rented child safety car seats to the disadvantaged in Carteret County, North Carolina, and Doris walked in and volunteered. "I had no idea who she was. We weren't in the office for more than twenty minutes when I thought, 'Oh my God, this woman could run any major corporation, and I have her renting car seats in Carteret County.' I was just fascinated by her. I didn't have any idea who Warren Buffett was. She was so interesting and so much fun. When I met her she had no money at all. She was clipping grocery coupons. I knew she had lost money. I knew she was watching her pennies."

They became close friends, and Diane later helped Doris through her battles with colon and endometrial cancer in 2002 and 2004.

When Doris inherited Berkshire Hathaway stock in 1996 and formed the Sunshine Lady Foundation, her first big action was to offer a million-dollar grant to the Carteret County Community Foundation, which they turned down. "Why? Because Doris wanted an audit, and also required 100 percent board involvement in fundraising. And they were terrified. They were very, very threatened by her. They didn't know what philanthropy was, and Doris didn't know what board responsibilities were. She fought her first battles here, and in some ways it was a great place to learn, because it wasn't on such a big scale. She taught this area the *meaning* of community because of the questions that she asked.

"She's taught me to be a real critical thinker," Diane said. "And after you know her, you can't sit on your hands anymore. She's changed my life immensely. I would never have been able to have the reward of helping kids without her."

Diane told a story about a young girl in Morehead City who was one of four daughters "totally neglected by their parents. No matter how hard she tried to win their approval, or how good her grades she got, they never acknowledged it. All she ever wanted, all she ever dreamed of was to teach school. We gave her a scholarship. She is now a third-grade teacher here in Carteret County. She's a fabulous teacher for any child who has any kind of gap in her life. And she's involved in the community, always in the newspaper running fundraisers. It's wonderful to see her living her dream and creating her own loving family, the family she should have had all along.

"And Doris is just the most fun person I've ever known," Diane said. "We've done some pretty outrageous things. She wanted to invest in changing lives, not spend money on luxuries for herself. But she did like diamonds, so she decided she would treat herself to a diamond from Borsheim's [a well-known jewelry store in Omaha owned by Berkshire Hathaway]. So she told me that Borsheim's was sending her some diamonds to see what she wanted to choose." Diane was dumbfounded that Borsheim's sent expensive gems and FedEx left the package on Doris' porch. Doris called Diane and asked her to come over. In the box were a six-carat diamond and a seven-carat diamond. I laid the diamonds on my finger and called my husband at work, and I said, 'I have thirteen carats of perfect diamonds on my fingers.' And he calmly said, 'You can't play with Doris anymore.' It was the one thing she did to treat herself."

MARY ELLEN BOX, *Scholarship Coordinator,* *Sunshine Lady Foundation*

Carolina Swamp Sauce brought Doris together with one of the first recruits for the Sunshine Lady Foundation and led to her meeting several others.

Mary Ellen Box met Doris in 1990 in Morehead City, North Carolina. "I was beginning a food manufacturing business; the parent company was a gourmet retail shop Doris frequented, looking for good chocolates. She spotted our products and liked the names and marketing—Carolina Swamp Stuff Inc. And she said, 'When you get ready to expand and look for investors, let me know.' We did, and we had a total of eight investors—four couples on the board— we worked really well together. I was CEO and COO, and she gave me one of Warren's annual reports to model my first one after.

"I'd been teaching. I had a master's in special education/ learning disabilities, but was always playing with food— catering, bartending, helping to start restaurants. The foods were cooking sauces and salad dressings with really funny names in the hopes that customers would cross-utilize them. They did and we were hugely successful, on QVC six times, tons of press and marketing awards, international distribution—coming from nothing. Doris helped with our first food show in D.C. We grew until the mid-1990s, reaching close to $1 million a year in sales. We decided to sell about the same time she was creating the Foundation."

She and her husband conducted the first national survey related to domestic violence workers' needs, and got the first check from the Foundation. Since Mary Ellen was soon to be semi-retired, Doris asked her to help her with the work.

Mary Ellen was sent to Duke University for training, and she drew on her business practices from Swamp Stuff to help decide about documentation and other policies. In earlier years, she'd worked in a residential facility for people with significant disabilities, and processed and doc- umented funding from Medicaid and Medicare. She also helped North Carolina develop early state-level interpreta- tion of new national education laws to govern how special education was to be run. But the governing principles of the Sunshine Lady Foundation, Mary Ellen said, are "common sense and humor."

"The first three years and $5 million we did from her living room and my office. I lived a block away and walked over each morning so we could put together the day's attack plan." She was also a part-time consultant for the new owners of Swamp Stuff, until it got so big they needed more help than Mary Ellen could manage while working for Doris. Several of the early staff, including Nancy Soward, who is now Executive Director of the Women's Independence Scholarship Program, were from her Swamp Sauce contacts.

After the third year, Doris brought in more help. Mary Ellen became part-time executive director while focusing on the scholarship program. During the first year of scholarship awards, the Foundation received a dozen applications, all of which were approved. "We have grown exponentially from that point," Mary Ellen said.

She said the Sunshine Lady Foundation does more than give young people money to go to college. It gets personally involved and does everything it can to give them what they need to succeed, including advice. For one thing, scholarship recipients must sign a pact promising they won't drink alcohol while in college. Mary Ellen was shattered in 2008 when a young woman in the program died in a car crash while intoxicated, and she broke down and cried at a meeting of recipients. She has become close to many of the scholarship recipients and stays in touch with them as they move ahead in their lives.

"You can pack up a poor kid and send him to a rich place, and if he's not equipped he's going to fail," she said. In our camp program, you can't send a kid to camp without them having proper clothes to wear. So we buy them the same kind of clothes the other kids wear. Not designer label stuff, but nice clothes, so the playing field is more even."

In the scholarship program, the Foundation determines "where you are right now and what you need to get to the next level, and what can we do to help you get ahead. I think she and I both wanted to remove any excuses, so we could help people to succeed in spite of themselves."

The scholarship program forbids wearing body-piercing jewelry or getting tattoos that are plainly visible for a reason. Doris wanted the students to be able to walk into her brother's office and get a job after they graduated from college. And they wouldn't be able to do that with a tattoo on the side of their head or a lip-piercing.

The Next Generation

During a recent visit to Davidson College in North Carolina, Doris was a combination of Gandhi, Santa Claus and Lucille Ball, transcendentally wise, unceasingly generous and self-effacingly funny. At colleges across the country, she is raising an army of young people who combine the joyous social consciousness of the 1960s with the clear-eyed efficiency and seriousness of the 1980s, minus the greed. This will be her legacy.

Some people in the current generation of philanthropists set up foundations to keep their relatives living the high life more than to help educate and heal those who need their help. Others waste a lot of time and money because they don't know what they're doing and they're not held accountable.

In an effort to reduce the amount of waste and inefficiency in philanthropy and help more of those in need more effectively, Doris launched the Sunshine Lady Foundation's Learning by Giving program at Davidson College in 2003. According to an IRS study, expenditures by nonprofits grew at twice the rate of the Gross Domestic Product from 1985 to 2004. In 2006, nonprofit revenues were roughly equivalent to those of the finance and insurance industries.

But few colleges were even considering preparing students to enter the field. That same year, nonprofit revenues represented ten percent of the GDP. And yet, in 2006, there were only four nonprofit programs for undergraduate students in the U.S, and all of them were partners of the Sunshine Lady Foundation's Learning by Giving program. By 2009, the relatively small Foundation, which led the way in this innovative concept, supported fifteen of forty-six such college programs in America. Doris, in her seventies and early eighties, was a visionary on the cutting edge of the trend.

The other college philanthropy courses she supports are at the University of Mary Washington, Cornell University, Tufts University, McMaster University in Ontario, the University of Montana, Valparaiso University, Ball State University, Georgetown University, Brandeis University, College of the Holy Cross, The University of California-Berkeley, the University of North Carolina at Chapel Hill, NYU and SUNY Binghamton.

Doris said the goal of Learning by Giving is to instill in students "the urge to do things for others all of their lives; to see the need to do something, to be an activist, to work toward social justice. The basis of every religion is, 'Do unto others as you would have them do unto you.'" She believes this program will not only outlive her, but also create a ripple effect that will inspire generations to come. When she visited Davidson in January 2010, the young people in that class, and those who had taken the class in the past and moved on to put what they learned to use at nonprofit organizations, vibrated like tuning forks, so filled were they with evangelical fervor about the power of making a difference.

"This is unquestionably the single most powerful and effective teaching tool I've ever been involved with," said

Davidson political science professor Ken Menkhaus. "It's real money, real projects, urgent social needs. The students are incredibly passionate about, engaged, and affected by this exercise. They learn core principles that they could never learn from a textbook, and it has been the most gratifying teaching experience in my career."

Menkhaus worked with Davidson student Sunbeams for several years before sitting down with Doris to talk about curriculum. Students learn the nuts and bolts of both philanthropic and nonprofit work, and they get an up close and personal look at the problems of their community and what it takes to have an impact by giving, including picking the spots where they can do the most good.

"The course is very popular with a wide range of our students," Davidson president Tom Ross said. "It builds on existing interest in nonprofit work, and it helps our students develop effective approaches to community development and advocacy. This course has changed lives—it has changed the lives of the Davidson students who've enrolled in the class, and it's changed the lives of the people to whom they have awarded grants. Doris Buffett, and her creativity in developing the idea, made this possible, and we are very grateful."

During her visit, Doris spoke to a group of alumni of the program, then she listened as one by one, they told stories of how she had changed the course of their lives in a way that was helping thousands of people far from the room. Georgia Krueger, Executive Director of the Ada Jenkins Center in Davidson, had tears in her eyes as she thanked her for starting her on a career track that led to her heading up an organization that provides education, health and family services for the area's needy. "It's all about making a difference in life," she said.

Her grandson, Alex, who coordinates this program "hopes that one of the things Doris Buffett would be remembered for would be her extreme passion for education and for trying to teach people how to do what she's doing and inspiring them."

Doris during a 2010 visit with Davidson College Learning by Giving students and alumni. BILL GIDUZ/DAVIDSON COLLEGE.

A Learning by Giving class at Cornell University.

ᗞEAR ᗞORIS

Some letters the Sunshine Lady Foundation receives are outrageously funny. One card from a man in Brooklyn was concise and to the point:

> *Deep in credit card debt: Could you write a check, payable to me, for $100,000? Please send to . . .*
> *Thanks so much!*

A very earnest letter from a Chinese woman living in Australia asked for funding to help her friend become the Antichrist:

> *We firstly met at a local church in Taiwan . . . At the beginning of knowing her, I felt that she was a little different from the people I knew . . . she told me there was only one occupation she is interested in, and that was being an Antichrist. Please be referred to the Book of Revelations in the Bible [Biblical prophecy says the Antichrist will trick humanity into believing it is being saved, then deny it the ultimate salvation] . . . She is an extremely smart girl. . . . However, she is still unemployed . . . she keeps preparing to carry out the duties of an Antichrist. She is not from a rich family and her only support from her granddad is about to*

end. I am writing this letter to ask financial support from you for this very special girl to help her have no worries as she prepares to be the Antichrist.

Sincerely . . .

A woman in Arkansas had simple needs:

. . . I would like to have 10 million dollars so that I can be self-sufficient and buy the things I would need to be on my own . . .

Your friend . . .

An enterprising high school senior in Florida came up with a proposal to help pay for college. He asked Doris to bid on Brutus, a 1,130-pound Angus steer he'd raised that was to be auctioned at the Central Florida Fair:

Should you purchase Brutus at auction, he will be taken to the butcher for you and packaged any way you desire.

Others are touching:

A grandmother with disabilities was physically abused by her daughter. She had been knocked down and kicked repeatedly. The consequences of the beating resulted in the grandmother's permanent need of a wheelchair. The Foundation took action to rid her of the abusive daughter, paid for a handicapped-accessible apartment for the grandmother, and furnished it so her six-year-old granddaughter could live with her. The young girl wrote in her own first grade handwriting:

Dear Sunshine Ladies,
Thank you so much for my bedroom.
I love it very much
It is so beautiful.

It's so big and cool.
I've never been in a bed that cool.
I am going to have a Tinkerbell bedroom.
Love, Ariel

P.S. I love you all. When you have time, write back.

Excerpts from some other letters:

♦ *I read in the paper about your gift and challenge to others to donate to FRAXA for Fragile X syndrome research. [Over $3.5 million was raised.] My wife and I are the parents of an 8-year-old boy, Ryan, who was diagnosed with Fragile X. I know with all my heart there is a "real boy" in there, much like the story of Pinocchio and Geppetto. He so much wants to be like the other children. With your donation and the strides that FRAXA is making every day, that hope is coming closer to reality.*

♦ *When I first started school, my oldest daughter wanted to work at Wendy's Restaurant. It was the only place she had seen people she knew make money. Now she wants to be an orthodontist. My next girl is determined to be a pharmacist. I know I could never have done this on my own. Thank you for believing in me, supporting me and cherishing me. I would love to meet you some day. I have to admit, I printed out your picture from the newsletter and keep it in my wallet. It reminds me someone is cheering me on.*

♦ *Thank you from the bottom of my heart for buying me a new glass eye. I had been without one for 36 years.*

When I get my new eye, I will mail you a picture of me and the eye.

♦ Every time I write to you I cry out of happiness, because it's not every day someone like me knows how it feels to be loved. I try not to remember my past because it hurts so much.

♦ It is so refreshing to know that there are people in this world who are willing to help another person and the only motive is to see that person succeed. While you have given me scholarship money, you have also given me something else . . . strength, courage and hope.

♦ I have wanted to be a nurse for many years, and my numerous hospital experiences when my son was being treated for a brain tumor reinforced that. I realize what real differences nurses can make and how they touch the lives of patients and their families. By leaving an abusive relationship and getting an education, I'm setting the best example I can for my children. Working full-time and raising a family including a child with a disability alone was not something I could do while attending college. Your scholarship has allowed me to go to school full time and be with my children.

♦ I've come full circle in understanding the cycle of violence, its impact on children and families across generations, and the gift of ending violence. I owe this in part to your willingness to reach out and make a difference in the lives of others through your generous educational donations. I often remark in lectures that if a woman has four children and each child does the same for 10 *generations, there will be nearly a million people as a result of the first union. If we change just one life, we have the potential to help millions in the process. Thanks for changing my life, Doris.*

♦ *I just can't thank you enough for this opportunity to change my future as well as my children's future. They are almost as excited as I am about my graduation. It will be so worth it to have them see what hard work and dedication can lead to. We live in an age of immediate gratification, and I, my children and my family have seen firsthand how dedicated someone has to be to reach an important goal.*

♦ *I am a social worker because you stood behind me and encouraged me. My life and the lives of my daughters have been changed forever because of the opportunities I've been given. I have a handwritten letter from my 13-year-old that calls me "Supermom." I take out that letter and read it out loud every chance I get because it makes me proud to know that my child sees me that way, and with that kind of encouragement, I can conquer the world. A friend calls me "Phoenix" because I rose from the ashes. I only hope the Foundation realizes the impact that you have had. Your faith in me has given me back my faith in myself.*

♦ *In 2003, I left an abusive relationship at age 43 with two children, then 4 and 3. If I had left that situation without your help, I would still be working a minimum-wage job, living in public housing and receiving government assistance. I knew there had to be something better, a way out, and it was higher education. The struggles victims of domestic violence endure, the fear it creates, can imprison them for life. As of 2009, thanks to your support, I have a master's degree in social work.*

- ◆ *Thank You. You are changing the world one family at a time.*

- ◆ *I would love to be able to follow your example in the future by encouraging and helping others in their lives.*

- ◆ *Please extend my gratitude to the wonderful staff who worked hard to make my success possible. May the Sunshine Lady Foundation expand day after day; may more women take advantage of this wonderful opportunity to free themselves from abuse and poverty and move on to a better life.*

NDEX